FOLENS
ENGLISH

DISCOVERIES

TERRY BROWN

MIKE FLEMING

Discoveries.

This book is intended to engage students in interesting and meaningful language and literature work within realistic contexts appropriate to 12 - 13 year old concerns.

There are 12 units, each one about a different subject. Every unit starts with a lead-in for all students and then encourages different activities for students working at widely different attainment levels. The text is presented as a double-page spread for ease of use, and is suitable for all abilities.

(1) Core activities are highlighted by the use of coloured circles, and there are extension activities for further work.

Extra support material for all the units can be found in the accompanying Teachers' book, all of which is photocopiable.

☆ A star symbol in the text indicates that relevant material is available to support weaker students, extend the advanced ones, as extra resources or to provide further structure to the work in the text. There are other sheets, not attached to units, aiming to correct common errors.

English is presented as a unified subject in which language work arises naturally and meaningfully in context. We have included complete texts rather than extracts where possible, and drawn on accessible works from major writers of the past.

Terry Brown
Mike Fleming

© 1990 Folens Limited, on behalf of the authors.

First published 1990 by Folens Limited, Dunstable and Dublin.

Folens Limited, Albert House, Apex Business Centre, Boscombe Road, Dunstable LU5 4RL, England.

ISBN 1 85276089-3

Printed in Singapore by Craft Print.

Contents

First impressions can easily be misleading. This unit is about the value of thinking carefully before you rush into making judgements about people you meet, places you visit, or things you read. You will also be talking about how to get started on your own writing.

In groups of four or five, look at the picture below for no more than 30 seconds each. Then shut the book. Give the picture a title and try to recall as many details as you can.

(1) Look at the picture again and see how well you remembered it and who in the group remembered particular details. Discuss what is "wrong" with the picture.

(2) The artist gave the title "*False Perspective*" to this picture which dates from 1754. Knowing the title helps us to "see" the picture the way the artist intended. Write a paragraph to go in a catalogue which will help people understand that the artist was deliberately making mistakes. Mention at least five of the mistakes in the picture. You will find that you need to do several drafts to get the paragraph sounding right.

Now try . . . . . .

3 Is **A** a drawing of a duck looking one way, or a
☆ rabbit looking the other? If you place a carrot in the picture it is likely to influence people's initial judgements. Can you you think of any games which illustrate how people's impressions of things can be influenced?

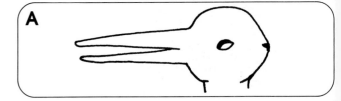

A

The following poem illustrates in an amusing way how our first impressions are not necessarily the ones to trust!

The Blind Men and The Elephant

It was six men of Indostan,
To learning much inclined,
Who went to see the Elephant
(Though all of them were blind),
That each by observation
Might satisfy his mind.

The first approached the Elephant,
And, happening to fall
Against his broad and sturdy side,
At once began to bawl,
"God bless me! but the Elephant
Is very like a wall!"

The second, feeling of the tusk,
Cried - "Ho! what have we here
So very round and smooth, and sharp?
To me 'tis mighty clear
This wonder of an Elephant
Is very like a spear!"

The third approached the animal
And happening to take
The squirming trunk within his hands,
Thus boldly up and spake:
"I see" - quoth he - "the Elephant
Is very like a snake!"

The fourth reached out his eager hand
And felt about the knee:
"What most this wonderous beast is like
Is mighty plain" quoth he "It is clear enough the Elephant
Is very like a tree!"

The fifth, who chanced to touch the ear,
Said - "E'en the blindest man
Can tell what this resembles most;
Defy the fact who can,
This marvel of an Elephant
Is very like a fan!"

The sixth no sooner had begun
About the beast to grope,
Than seizing on the swinging tail
That fell within his scope,
"I see" - quoth he - "the Elephant
Is very like a rope!"

And so these men of Indostan
Disputed loud and long,
Each in his own opinion
Exceeding stiff and strong,
Though each was partly in the right,
And all were in the wrong!

John G. Saxe

④ In your group prepare to read the poem aloud. Decide how you are going to divide the reading in the group and which parts you will emphasise. Can you devise a mime to go with the reading to make it more entertaining?

⑤ Imagine that this poem is being read at an assembly followed by an explanation of its "moral". Write a paragraph which explains what the point behind the poem is.

⑥ Try the same idea in a written piece of your own. It does not have to be a poem. Decide on an object which can be perceived in different ways - an animal, a tree, a car, etc. - and decide which parts you are going to describe.

1.2 Impressions of People.

The first impressions we form of people we meet can easily be influenced by our preconceptions, i.e. by what we assume about them before we meet them. If we are told something about somebody in advance it can easily influence what we think.

Imagine that Jane is a new pupil in a school. Below are two different descriptions of her.

A

"Jane is really stuck up. She's a terrible snob. Her family are very rich and she loves to brag about them! She is also very bossy. She likes to get her own way and sulks if she doesn't. Whatever you do, do not mention food - she's a real glutton and eats like a pig."

B

"Jane is very friendly but she is a bit shy. She just moved here recently. She is from quite a large family and they do some very interesting things. Jane is a very honest person and likes to say what she thinks. She's also very generous and a good friend."

Imagine that Nimesh had the following conversation with Jane.

N: Hello. You're new in this school aren't you?
J: Yes, I am.
N: When did you move into the area?
J: Not long ago.
N: Do you live near here? Does it take you long to get to school?
J: A few miles - my father drops me off on his way to work.
N: What sort of car does he have?
J: It's a Porsche - you could see it tomorrow if you're interested in cars.
N: Thanks. Do you have any brothers or sisters?
J: Yes, I've got three brothers. They are all older than me. One works for a film studio, one lives in France and the other one is a professional footballer - well an apprentice I should say - he's not played in any matches yet.
N: There's a school match on this evening. Perhaps you would like to go with me and watch it. We're in the final.
J: No thanks, I don't really like watching football. I could see you after it though.
     Maybe we could get something to eat. Would you like one of these? (offers a sweet)

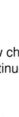

(**1**) Nimesh is writing about his first meeting with Jane in a letter to a friend. Write two versions, one of which could have been influenced by what **A** said to him and one which might have been influenced by what **B** said.

(**2**) Who was right, **A** or **B**? It would all depend on the TONE of voice used by Jane and any GESTURES which accompanied what she said. Read the short piece of conversation in two different ways to show the different interpretations.

(**3**) Now choose which interpretation you prefer and continue the conversation when they next meet.

People also make assumptions about other people by using stereotypes, that is they assume that one group of people all have the same characteristics. Women, men and people of different races are the groups most commonly stereotyped but it can happen to all sorts of people. Make a chart in these columns, listing the group of people, a common stereotype of them and an individual you know (or invent), to counteract the stereotype.

☆

Group	Stereotype	Individual I know
Women	dainty, giggly, not serious, worried about appearance	Mary Henshaw - manager of local engineering factory
American tourists		
old people		

Impressions of people are also formed by their appearances. Look at the photographs on this page and select the occupations and the moods and match them to the pictures. (Answers on page 96.)

BAR-WORKER   TEACHER

HEAD TEACHER

ENGINEER   NURSE   STORE MANAGER   DOCTOR

DETECTIVE

EMBARRASSED

ANGRY

PUZZLED

CROSS   HAPPY

SURPRISED

PLEASED   THOUGHTFUL

1.3 Images.

It is always worth thinking twice before jumping to conclusions about people. The same is true when forming impressions of objects, animals and insects. Read the following passage about Jacob.

Jacob enjoyed himself torturing and killing flies. He tore off their wings and legs, and then watched with pleasure their helpless efforts to escape from him. Sometimes he collected a number of them together, and crushed them at once to death; glorifying, like many a famous hero, in the violence he was doing to them. His brother asked him again and again to stop, but it did no good. He could not persuade him to believe that flies are capable of pain, and have a right, like ourselves, to life, freedom and enjoyment. The signs of agony which they express by the twistings and writhings of their bodies he did not understand, and would not consider.

Alex had a microscope; and one day he asked Jacob to examine a most beautiful and surprising animal. "Look", he said, "how it is studded from head to tail with black and silver, and its body is all covered with bristles. The head has got a pair of lovely eyes, encircled with silver hairs; and the trunk consists of two parts, which fold over each other.

The whole body is decorated with plumes which are more dazzling than the dress in the courts of the greatest princes." Jacob was amazed and delighted with what he saw, and wanted to know the name of this wonderful animal. It was taken from the microscope; and when he looked at it with his naked eye, he saw that it was one of the flies which had been the victims of his cruelty.

① Why should we worry about killing disease-carrying flies? Some people say flies are creatures like any other. Why should we kill them? What are your views? Present them to a small group or the rest of the class.

② Write a similar description of your own starting with first impressions and then giving a more considered view based on a closer inspection. Try with something small - insects, weeds, etc. - or write alternative descriptions of something larger like a building.

Now try . . . . . .

3 Make a display of pictures and text called "Don't judge a book by its cover".
  ● Collect pictures from different places and give them two different titles which change their meanings completely. For example, an advertisement for an expensive car could be given the title, "Lead Pollution Kills".
  ● Try to find pictures of people at work which break stereotypes.
  ● Include a few stories.

☆ **REMINDER - Semi-colons.**

The semi-colon is used quite frequently in the passage about Jacob. It is a form of punctuation which is useful when you want to write two sentences which are linked in terms of meaning but which cannot be linked by a comma because they are complete sentences. (If you are not sure of the rule for using commas, you should revise this.) If in doubt do not use a semi-colon because a fullstop will always do in its place.

Look carefully at the following examples:

The new teacher seemed to the class stern, unpleasant and distant; the children were too young to recognise his uncertainty and nervousness.

The film star gave the impression of youth, vitality and glamour; in real life you could see the wrinkles of age and stress under the make-up.

Invent similar "First Impression" sentences.

Poets often help us to see things in new and interesting ways. They can help us form a fresh view of objects and scenes which have become familiar to us. Not many poems, however, can be fully understood just on one brief reading, the way you might read a gripping short story. But poems really do repay the effort of looking again and thinking about the meaning. The following poem by Craig Raine is well worth considering in some detail.

A Martian Sends A Postcard Home

Caxtons are mechanical birds with many wings
and some are treasured for their markings -

they cause the eyes to melt
or the body to shriek without pain.

I have never seen one fly, but
sometimes they perch on the hand.

Mist is when the sky is tired of flight
and rests its soft machine on ground:

then the world is dim and bookish
like engravings under tissue paper.

Rain is when the earth is television.
It has the property of making colours darker.

Model T is a room with the lock inside -
a key is turned to free the world

for movement, so quick there is a film
to watch for anything missed.

But time is tied to the wrist
or kept in a box, ticking with impatience.

In homes, a haunted apparatus sleeps,
that snores when you pick it up.

If the ghost cries, they carry it
to their lips and soothe it to sleep

with sounds. And yet, they wake it up
deliberately, by tickling with a finger.

Only the young are allowed to suffer
openly. Adults go to a punishment room

with water but nothing to eat.
They lock the door and suffer the noises

alone. No one is exempt
and everyone's pain has a different smell.

Now try . . . . . .

4   In pairs or groups go through the poem,
     discussing each pair of lines in turn and
     thinking about the image - the picture in your
     mind - that the poet has created.

5   Copy the poem in the centre of a sheet of
☆   paper and surround it with sketches which
     would help a reader understand the various
     images.

1.4 Writing.

You could complete this unit with a piece of extended writing of your own choice called "First Impressions". Here are some suggestions:

- a general piece about the need not to jump to conclusions too quickly
- a story which includes stereotyping
- an account of your first impressions of your school
- a friend
- your class
- a building you know
- an account written by an alien who has visited the earth for the first time.

When you start to write do you often feel stuck and not sure how to start? Perhaps you are trying to start before you have given yourself enough time to sort out your ideas. It is usually not a good idea to start with a large, fresh piece of paper with a neat title and your pen ready at the top left hand corner! That can easily inhibit you from writing anything! You might like to try these stages instead.

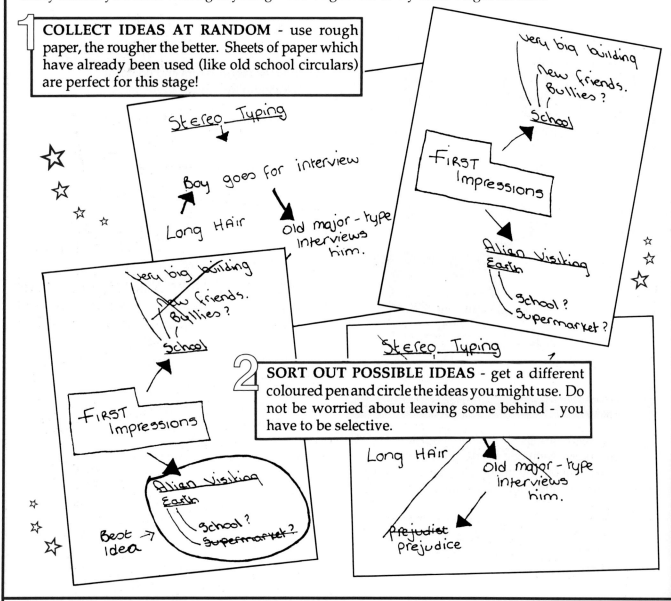

1 **COLLECT IDEAS AT RANDOM** - use rough paper, the rougher the better. Sheets of paper which have already been used (like old school circulars) are perfect for this stage!

2 **SORT OUT POSSIBLE IDEAS** - get a different coloured pen and circle the ideas you might use. Do not be worried about leaving some behind - you have to be selective.

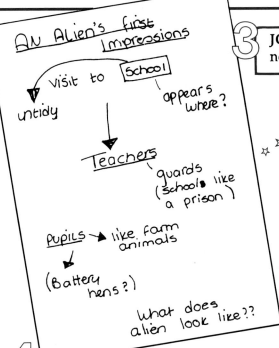

An Alien's first Impressions

visit to [School]

untidy

appears where?

Teachers

guards (schools like a prison)

PUPILS → like farm animals

(Battery hens?)

What does alien look like??

3 JOT DOWN IDEAS IN MORE DETAIL - add notes to expand the ideas you are going to use.

Alien Story outline

Arrival in library

(alien disguised as Cactus?

very quiet

no one notices)

Entrance of Pupils (in silence) — teacher comes in

SHOUTING

fear —

Alien feels sorry for them

Pupils not doing work — (drawing pictures of teacher)

Alien thinks this is what all schoolwork consists of.

pto.

4 WORK OUT AN OUTLINE - sort out your ideas into some rough sort of order - you may change your mind later but it helps to have some sort of idea about what you are going to do in the entire piece.

Now...

5 WRITE A VERY ROUGH PRIVATE DRAFT - this one is only for you to see. Just scribble your thoughts down quickly.

6 WRITE YOUR FIRST DRAFT "proper". You may write several drafts and get other people to read and advise before you are satisfied.

My first mission to the newly discovered planet Earth had started. I arrived in a large, cold room. It was very quiet. I had not been told where I was going - Just told to find out how the Human people treat and look after their young young. I waited for a bit. I could not see any young Humans then the door opened and in came lots of them all in a line they didn't look happy. Then In Come a Human bigger than the rest he was. Shouting, the young looked at him in fear, I didn't understand why he should be shouting at them. He was being really horrible to them I was told Earth was a Happy Place but not hear here.

Emily martindale.

My first mission to the newly discovered planet Earth had started. I arrived in a large, cold room. It was very quiet. I had not been told where I was going - Just told to find out how the Human people treat and look after their young. But I think It is called a school.

I waited for a while. I could not

2.1 Likes and Dislikes.

In this unit you will be thinking about individual likes and dislikes and exploring how writers use language to convey particular feelings.

You and two friends have just won a competition. The prize is that for one day you can do whatever you like. Money is no object - the organisers will pay all costs. With your two partners, plan your day. Remember, it must last no more than twenty four hours, and you have to stay together.

1 *How much I enjoy*
the scent of rain on soil
after a dry spell.
Write some three line verses of your own. The first line is always the same; the second explains what it is you enjoy; the third line comments on it in some way.
How much I enjoy
a visit to the dentist,
when it's all over!

Now try . . . . . .

2 Find poems and other passages which show someone else's enthusiasms. Look at sports writing, articles in magazines or poetry books.

Have you ever liked someone but found it difficult to let them know?

Lizzie

When I was eleven
there was Lizzie.
I used to think this

You don't care, Lizzie,
you say that you're a ginger-nut
and you don't care.

I've noticed
that they try to soften you up

they say
you're clumsy
they say
you can't wear shorts
to school

but you say
"I don't care,
I mean
how can I play football
in a skirt?"

Lizzie,
I'm afraid of saying
I think you're great
because, you see,
the teachers call you
tomboy.

I'm sorry
but I make out, as if
I agree with the teachers

and the other girls
wear bracelets
and I've noticed
they don't shout like you
or whistle
and, you see,
the other boys
are always talking about
those girls
with the bracelets

So I do too.
So I know
that makes me a coward
but that's why I don't dare
to say you're great,

but I think to myself
when you're there

I just try to show
I like you
by laughing
and joking about
and pulling mad faces.

I'm sorry
but I don't suppose
you'll ever know...

Michael Rosen

(3) Imagine that the author wrote this poem in
private and it was found by Lizzie. She left a
similar poem in his desk for him to find. Write
out a poem in reply in the same style using short
lines and no rhyme. You could start as follows:
*I found a poem
and I wrote back this:*

(4) Analyse friendship groups in your class. Start
with yourself and your friends as in the diagram.
Go on to their friends and gradually build up an
analysis. The closer you place the names, the
closer the friends. Arrows show if the friendship
is a one or two-way affair.
● Discover reasons for the friendships.
● Do friends share hobbies or interests?

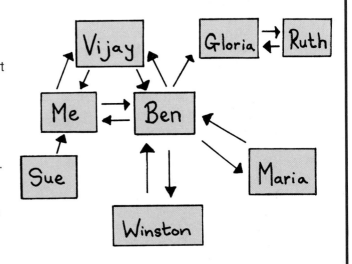

2 Young 2 Go 4 Grils.

M r Timpson came to Davenport Secondary for a term as a student teacher, to help Mr Roonie with lower school geography. He was very earnest and nervous, wore jeans, open sandals and no socks, and was very inclined to blush. If Melanie Fish happened to stand next to him in the dinner queue, for example, and greeted him with a friendly, "Hi, Sir", well, that was enough to send him rosy to the roots of his hair, no problem. Meena Patel and Sharon Marriott of the second year thought he looked cute when he blushed and they were always trying to set him off. But he was getting better at taking deep breaths as the weeks went by, and controlling his blushes.

Meena Patel and Sharon Marriott were called the Siameses by the other second years. This was because they did everything and had everything the same. If they liked a teacher, then they always liked the same one (as in the case of Mr Timpson). When Meena had a fluffy orange pencil case with plastic eyes that winked at you, then Sharon had to have one. When Sharon had an autograph album (Macdonald tartan - wipeable - with a tasselled pencil) Meena had one too (only hers was red Moroccan leather with "autograph album" printed across the front in gold).

They both launched their albums on the same day at the same time - the beginning of Mr Timpson's geography lesson. With any luck someone - say, Christopher Crutchley - would write something rude on them and Mr Timpson would ask to see what was being passed around the classroom. Then he'd blush.

The first person to write on Meena's album was Sharon:

Memories will fade, Leaves may dry,
My friendship with you, Will never die.

And the first person to write something on Sharon's book was Meena:

There's big ships, and little ships,
But the best ships, Is friendships.

Next they passed their books to Caroline Stewart:

There's a man lives down our street,
He's got no hair but he's got three feet.

Who passed them to Stephanie Bishop:

Teacher, teacher, I declare,
Tarzan's lost his underwear.

Who passed them to Brian Turley:

I eat my peas with honey,
I've done it all my life,
It makes the peas taste funny,
But it keeps them on the knife.
Signed: Brian Turley. Friend of the Earth.

Brian Turley was new to Davenport that term. He was skinny and eager and good at lessons, and, in Christopher Crutchley's eyes at least, too innocent for his own well being. Early on, Christopher had scrawled across Brian Turley's geography book "2 Young 2 Go 4 Grils".

The next person to have the albums after Brian Turley was Fergie Fish.

Fergie gave careful thought to the claims of each girl on his attention before committing himself to their albums. He scrutinized them across the room. Meena, he decided after a moment or two, was all right. In fact she was ten out of ten, A One Plus, and he couldn't think why he hadn't noticed this before - so she got:

Meena bent to pick a rose,
She was so sweet and slender,
Meena bent to pick a rose,
And ping went her suspender.

Whereas Sharon Marriott had always been slow to appreciate the charms of Fergie Fish:

Roses are red, Violets are blue,
With a face like yours, You should be in a zoo.

Fergie then passed the albums to Christopher Crutchley. He had a great deal of time for Chris these days. He was more grown up than Tez and given to remarks like "I am a man" and "I know these things" while tapping the side of his nose, and Fergie considered he might well pick up some handy hints from that direction. There were days when Fergie thought that Chris Crutchley was his favourite mate.

On the other hand Chris Crutchley was Mr Timpson's least favourite pupil. This wasn't surprising. He was more or less the least favourite pupil of every teacher in Davenport.

"Chris!" whispered Fergie. "Chri-is!" his eyes darted to the front with every whisper. (Although inclined to nervousness, Mr Timpson did have his more positive side!)

Christopher didn't hear. He was partially deaf at the best of times and on top of this had just removed his hearing aid. He was deeply engrossed in his geography exercise book. Where Mr Timpson had written "This is very poor work", Chris had written "Thank you", and where Mr Timpson had written "THIS IS REALLY ATROCIOUS", Chris had written "Thank you very much".

Fergie watched Mr Timpson turn to the board, did a quick calculation, dived across the gangway, tapped Christopher Crutchley on the shoulder, wiggled his eyebrows in the direction of the albums, dived back into his seat, snatched up a pencil and was scrutinizing the blackboard with knitted-browed concentration - all before Mr Timpson turned round.

Thus prompted, Christopher Crutchley transferred his attention to the autograph albums. He thought for a moment, then scrawled across a blue page in Sharon's:

Don't make love on the garden gate,
Love may be blind but the neighbours ain't.

Then he began to scratch the same on Meena's. "CHERRISTOPHER CERRUTCHLEY!"

Whistling to himself, Christopher carried right on scrawling. He hadn't heard a thing. Nor did he notice Mr Timpson regarding him with irritation and twitching the small microphone all teachers wore round their necks like a mayoral chain when trying to pass on knowledge to Christopher Crutchley.

There was a swift displacement of air - Mr Timpson bearing down on Christopher like the avenging angel and forcibly replacing the hearing aid. His voice crackled and boomed from somewhere directly above Christopher's head. Christopher winced.

"I was just saying, Crutchley, that next week is PLANT A TREE WEEK," bellowed Mr Timpson. "This is the most important time of the year for TREE PEOPLE. Planting trees is something ECOLOGISTS are interested in. Do you know what ECOLOGY means Crutchley?"

Christopher didn't. He glared.

Brian Turley beamed up at Mr Timpson. "I do, Sir. Ecologists are the greens, Sir, I'm a green." He went on to explain. Mr Timpson looked gratified. If Christopher was generally agreed to be the least desirable pupil in the second year, Brian Turley was fast establishing himself as the most favoured. He was happy to learn whatever teachers chose to teach, with a bias towards any project that involved planting,

growing, nurturing and conservation. Biology and geography were his best subjects.

Meanwhile Christopher had remembered his clinic card. Whenever a member of staff recalled the hearing aid Christopher had a back-up system of problem zones requiring urgent attention. He shoved his way between bags and legs to the front. "Sorry, Sir. Only just remembered, Sir, I'm due at t'clinic twenty past. Me verruca, Sir."

Mr Timpson scrutinized the clinic card. "This signature of the headmaster's wouldn't happen to be a forgery, would it, Crutchley?"

Christopher looked outraged and vigorously shook his head. "I swear on me mother's Bible, Sir."

"I'll send it along to the headmaster all the same, just to make sure."

Christopher snatched it off him, muttering something and ploughed his way back to his desk.

"And don't kick Brian Turley like that."

"I didn't kick 'im, Sir! I jus' poked 'im with me foot."

Back at his desk Christopher brooded. He'd get that know-all Turley! He soothed his injured pride by going through his excuse notes. These all followed the same format but the variations were endless. "Christopher must not do woodwork/basketball/ athleticks/musick as he has a soar thum/weak rists/ strained tendum/perfrated ear drum." Plus a note diagnosing a rare but galloping variety of athlete's foot to get him off showers. None of them'd get him off geography, though - not now Mr Timpson had blown his clinic card. He'd get that Timpo as well!

Fergie had seized on the diversion of the clinic card to return the albums to Meena and Sharon. They were disappointed at first to see them come back. Mr Timpson had neither confiscated them nor blushed, which had been the objects of the exercise.

But when Sharon read what Fergie had written in her book she went scarlet - with fury! Meena was blushing too - with pleasure - and grinning. Sharon snatched her friend's album and compared her own Fergie entry with Meena's. Then she accidently-on-purpose dropped Meena's album on the floor and stuck her foot on it. The result was a scuff mark. Sharon scrawled across it, "SHAZ WOZ HERE".

When Meena saw what Sharon had done she went redder still. She seized Sharon's book and wrote across the page in angry orange letters, "YOU ARE A CHICKY GIRL". This didn't seem nearly harsh enough so she turned up another page and wrote, "YOU ARE A NICETY WITCH". When the bell went Mr Timpson left the classroom as even complexioned and cool as when he'd come in. It was Sharon and Meena who left with a very high colour.

Such a friendship couldn't remain in fragments for long, though. The girls were soon reunited. For one thing, since the day of the autograph albums, Christopher Crutchley and Fergie Fish had started fancying one of each of them. Fergie had taken to staring at the crisp white cuffs of Meena's school blouse and the piece of twisted black cotton she wore round one slim wrist and sighing to himself. And Chris decided that Sharon Marriott who took on the teachers and wore sweat bands to lessons was just the girl for him. But as far as the girls were concerned, one admirer each was one too many. Now if one lad had fancied both of them, they'd have been able to fuss and swoon over the same lad, like at the moment they fussed and swooned over Mr Timpson.

Fergie and Christopher found it hard to accept that those they had fancied didn't fancy them, and took it out on Brian Turley. They'd sing in unison whenever they saw him coming:

"What's skinny and keen, and ever so GREEN?"
"A Turley!"

Meanwhile, Christopher hadn't forgotten he'd sworn vengeance on Brian Turley and Mr Timpson - it was just that he hadn't hit on a plan yet. But when he received his half-term grades and compared them with Brian Turley's, dreams of revenge grew sweet. Even Fergie was a bit put out when he compared his grades with Turley's. He told Mr Timpson so at the beginning of geography. "Attainment D Effort D -! I'm sorry, Sir, you'll have to go!"

Mr Timpson eyed him grimly. "It's not that you couldn't do better, as you know very well. Persistent misuse of the head, Fergus, that's your problem."

Fergie ignored this. "It's the last lesson before half-term today, y'know, Sir. Can we play murderball?"

Brian Turley frowned, "Oh, no, Sir. I want lessons."

Fergie turned on him. "Well I want murderball so you can shut it." Fergie looked pleadingly at Mr Timpson.

"That'll do Fish."

"Oh go on, Sir. All the teachers play summat with us before a holiday." He omitted to say this was only at the end of full term and was usually fizz buzz. "S'nothing to it, Sir, honest. You just, like, shove all the desks together 'cept for four, for goals, and borrow a cricket ball from Mr Mortimer and ..."

"I said that'll do."

As it turned out the lessons were interrupted anyway. Meena and Sharon groaned when it happened. They'd discovered it was Mr Timpson's birthday and wanted to bring him out in a record breaking blush. They'd found just the card for the job too. They'd been a bit miserable even before the interruption. It was half-term already - only a few more weeks and Mr Timpson'd lope, blushing, out of their lives for ever, and who were they going to fuss and swoon over when Mr Timpson left? And now it looked as if they were going to be done out of their Mount Vesuvius of a half-term blush.

It was the head who interrupted them, delivering a visitor. The arrival of the headmaster alone, fresh back to school and minus his appendix, would have proved enough to send Mr Timpson a light magenta. Meena and Sharon recognised this and cheered up.

"We have a visitor this morning," gulped Mr Timpson when the head had left. He was growing rosier every second. "This is ..."

But the visitor held up his hand. "No need to tell them, Mr ... They all know who I am. I'm something of a celebrity in this locality, mmm, children, am I not?" He beamed down upon the second years who stared blankly back. Meena threw her eyebrows up at Sharon who gave an expressive shrug.

Christopher Crutchley was one of the few who did know who he was - Monty Pendlebury, the local M.P. He knew because his dad was for ever inviting him to table a motion on behalf of the Crutchleys.

"Put your hands up, children, those who know who I am." Mr Pendlebury moved majestically down one of the aisles so that those who couldn't quite make their minds up could get an all-round view. Mr Timpson, not thinking straight, followed him.

Christopher Crutchley glimpsed his opportunity. He leaned across to Brian Turley. "Do you know who that is?"

Brian shook his head, looking worried. Christopher whispered in his ear. Brian thanked Christopher warmly and stuck up his hand.

Mr Monty Pendlebury swung suddenly on his heel, nearly sending Mr Timpson flying. He strutted to the front. Most of the children by now were sticking their hands half up, then lowering them again if the celebrity happened to look in their direction. Mr Timpson, sensing that the honour of the school was at stake, inclined his head slightly in the direction of Brian Turley. He didn't wish to influence the member of parliament's choice, of course. But at least from that quarter due seriousness and accuracy could be guaranteed.

Luckily Mr Pendlebury took the hint. He laid a friendly hand on Brian's thin hair. "Well little man, who is it you have standing in front of you this morning?"

Brian smiled up in delight. "The nit man, sir!"

Both Mr Timpson and Mr Pendlebury turned a very deep ruby. And Mr Timpson continued to glow forth like a peony at dusk long after the visitor had taken his disgusted leave. Meena reported that she'd taken a peep at his sandals. Even his big toes had blushed!

Christopher didn't get to hear what the M.P. had said to Brian Turley. He'd been modifying his hearing aid lately so that it cut out at his bidding. Unfortunately, nowadays, it sometimes did it of its own accord.

The outcome wasn't quite what Christopher had expected either. When Brian Turley discovered the extent of his error he proved himself a far more fiery blusher than Mr Timpson'd ever been. Meena and Sharon beheld him with fascination and enthusiasm. No question now who would be their pet when Mr Timpson left. "2 Young 2 Go for Grils" was now "hot favourite" and a half!

When Mr Timpson and Brian Turley had cooled down a bit, Sharon and Meena wished their former love many happy returns of the day and presented him with his card. It was a pink card inside a pink envelope. On the front it said "Hoping this finds you 'in the pink' on your birthday" and it showed a shock-headed blond winking at him through a window. You opened the window when you opened the card.

And as soon as Mr Timpson looked inside he was 'in the pink' all over again! The blond was winking at him from her bath tub. She was sitting bolt upright, not entirely covered in soap bubbles, and pink as a newly peeled prawn!

In this story, by Susan Gregory, characters seem to spend their time switching between liking and disliking each other. It only seems to take one small trigger to set them off in one direction or the other.

1 Take one character and then look for the information you need by skim-reading the story.
● Pick out every part where we are told that person likes or dislikes another person.
● Name the other person and give the reason.
● Try this for EITHER Sharon OR Meena. Then try it for EITHER Christopher OR Fergie.
● How do your two lists compare?
● Is the writer being fair to both boys and girls or does she treat one sex more sympathetically than the other?
● Is life in the second form REALLY like this?

2 If you were to choose someone from the second form at Davenport to be your friend, whom would you choose and why?

3 The person about whom we learn the most is Christopher Crutchley. Imagine he were to apply for a part-time job. He asked Mr Timpson to act as his referee. Mr Timpson is very honest and very fair. He would write a full and truthful account of Christopher.
● Using only what you learn about Christopher from this story, write Mr Timpson's reference. Start off: *I have known Christopher Crutchley since I came to teach at Davenport at the start of this term.*

2.3 Off My Chest.

Your local radio station has a weekly programme called *Off My Chest*. The idea is that each week listeners are invited to write in about something that has made them angry.

1 Write your own letter for possible inclusion in the next programme. Be careful to set it out correctly - the producer only considers correct letters.

2 ☆ Your class has been chosen for a Special Edition of this programme.
It is to be a half-hour show with letters read out by their writers, and discussed in turn by a small panel of invited guests.
You will need:
- A small editorial group to choose which letters are to be used and to edit them.
- A chairperson for the programme.
- A panel of three who will listen to each letter and suggest what might be done.
The rest of the class will be the audience and letter-writers.

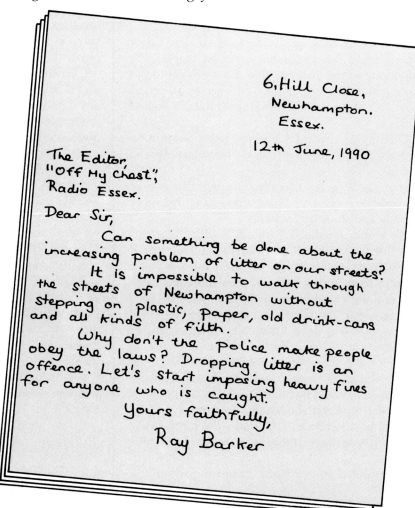

6, Hill Close,
Newhampton.
Essex.

12th June, 1990

The Editor,
"Off My Chest",
Radio Essex.

Dear Sir,

Can something be done about the increasing problem of litter on our streets?
It is impossible to walk through the streets of Newhampton without stepping on plastic, paper, old drink-cans and all kinds of filth.
Why don't the police make people obey the laws? Dropping litter is an offence. Let's start imposing heavy fines for anyone who is caught.

Yours faithfully,

Ray Barker

Noise is a subject which makes many people angry. When you are listening to loud pop music it may be difficult to understand how it is that other people do not share your enthusiasm! In our crowded island we are continually finding that what one person does as a hobby annoys someone else. It is not just a matter for compromise, either. Quiet pop music just is not the same, is it? And it can still be annoying!

Now try . . . . . .

3 In pairs, choose an activity which is liked by one person and disliked by another. Role play a telephone conversation in which one is complaining to the other. Each of you could then write down brief notes outlining your case. A third person could suggest a compromise. Does the compromise satisfy either of you? Would it work?

4 Carry out a survey among the class, friends and relatives, to find out people's pet likes and dislikes. Restrict everyone to two of each and display the results in chart form.

5 ☆ Find out what hobbies are enjoyed in the class and prepare talks about them.

The language people use to describe something can tell you what they are feeling about it. One person describes music as "loud", another as "blaring". "Loud" is a neutral word, but "blaring" indicates that the noise is offensive.

(6) Adjectives that people use often show us what they think. Work out replacements for the adjectives here which will then indicate dislike of whatever it is. The first one is done for you.

Driving a car at a FAST speed	**breakneck** speed
Painting a house in BRIGHT colours	
Going on a LONG walk	
Singing in a LOUD voice	

We can take this further. When people sell secondhand goods, they are usually careful to emphasise the best points, and perhaps not to mention the bad ones. They want you to like what you imagine they are selling. "Charming country cottage in beautiful location. Minimum amenities. Ideal for conversion." This could be a broken-down shack, miles from anywhere! "Minimum amenities" might mean no gas, electricity, mains water or sewerage, just a nearby stream and an earth closet. We call this speaking - or writing - *euphemistically*. "Minimum amenities" is *a euphemism* - a polite way of saying something.

(7) You have been given the task of selling the following. Work out *euphemistic* ways of describing them so that they sound attractive but don't lie about them!
● An electric railway set which is scratched, bent, and hasn't worked for years.
● A teenage doll with no hair, one arm missing, and several sets of torn clothes.
● A stereo record player with no stylus and only one loudspeaker.
● A set of scratched 45" records from the 1970s.

Now try . . . . . .

8 You have seen the following advertisements in your local free paper. You are a cynical kind of person, so you don't expect them to be quite as they sound. Write down what you MIGHT expect them to be like, giving as much detail as you can.

FOR SALE

Compact family tent with 2 almost complete inner tents. Zip and seams need some attention.
Set of toys and games suitable age 7-11. In reasonable condition, though not all complete. To be sold as a set - no splitting.
Boy's bike (suit 11-14 years) in good running order. 5 gears (need adjusting), lighting set, rear carrier. Rust negligible.

---

9 If an advertisement is really misleading, you can complain about it. In pairs imagine you are in charge of a local free advertising paper. Suggest a simple set of rules to control the standard of advertisements.

3.1 Fear.

In this unit you will be thinking about fear and what it does to people. You will also be considering how stories are constructed.

(1) Which of the following would you find frightening? Some are real, others simply the content of imagination, dreams or films. List them in order placing the one you would find most frightening at the top and so on. How do your reactions compare with those of the class as a whole?

Now try . . . . . .

2   In groups discuss what sorts of things frighten you. How much agreement is there? Again, make a list showing if there is any agreement in the group.

3   Cast your mind back to your early childhood. Can you think of anything which frightened you then because you did not understand it? For example, being frightened of cats' eyes in the road, thinking they were real cats. There is a well known story about a boy who is frightened of the pig-man (the man who empties the food bins) because he thinks the man is half man and half pig.

4 ☆   Devise a simple survey to try on other people to discover what are the most common fears people have. This could be in the form of a questionnaire or interview. You could try making you own collage to accompany it.

Read the following passage which comes as the climax in a story.

Ben was standing on a narrow ledge fifty feet up a sheer rock face.

For the first time, Ben looked down. Making sure his feet were firmly on the ledge and his hands were safely gripping the rock, he turned his head very slowly, looked down past his feet, and focused his eyes on the distant ground fifty feet below.

He looked quickly up again and shut his eyes. His fingers scraped for a firmer grip so that, although he didn't notice, they began to bleed. His brain reeled and he opened his eyes to steady himself. His own heartbeat threatened to choke him as he felt the sweat of fear trickling down his body. His knees were actually shaking and he was in danger of falling into that appalling void, indeed a panic desire seemed to be pulling him towards it.

He tried to concentrate on the rock face a few inches in front of his eyes. He could see it in minute detail, the rough texture, individual colours, and tiny crevices where the lichen was growing. He knew his only chance was to become calm, stay in control, and think carefully how he could climb down. He breathed deeply and tried to approach the task, stage by stage, fighting always against the panic which threatened to engulf him.

At that moment he dislodged a small boulder which crashed heavily down the rock face until, after what seemed an age, it thudded into the ground below. Ben let go an involuntary sob of sheer terror and pressed his whole body against the rock face.

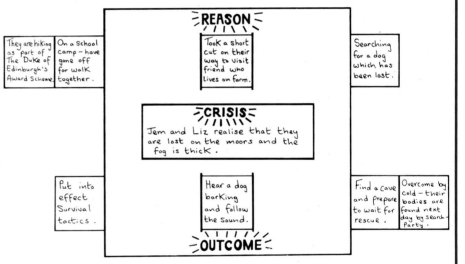

REASON

They are hiking as part of The Duke of Edinburgh's Award Scheme.

On a school camp – have gone off for walk together.

Took a short cut on their way to visit friend who lives on farm.

Searching for a dog which has been lost.

CRISIS

Jem and Liz realise that they are lost on the moors and the fog is thick.

Put into effect Survival tactics.

Hear a dog barking and follow the sound.

Find a cave and prepare to wait for rescue.

Overcome by cold – their bodies are found next day by search party.

OUTCOME

(5) When we are very frightened, we experience physical changes. Make notes listing the physical changes in Ben. Add your own notes about any other physical changes you have experienced when you have been frightened. Keep these notes as you will be using them later.

(6) This is the CRISIS of Ben's story, the moment when either he loses control or he doesn't. How he resolves the crisis will decide the ending. But first it is necessary to decide how he got into this situation.

(7) Decide what caused Ben to try to climb the rock face despite his fear of heights? When you have made your choice, write some notes saying what happened up to the moment our extract begins. Share your reasons with the rest of the class and decide whether each one is believable. Are there other possibilities that could have made him start the climb?

(8) Next, it is necessary to resolve the crisis. There are many different things that could happen, so try to think beyond the obvious. Decide what is going to happen in your version and again make notes so that you can share the ideas.

(9) Now collect all the reasons that people in the class have invented, and all the outcomes, and display them on a diagram as in the illustration. Are there any particular combinations which might be more effective?

3.2 Out of Control.

When our fear is out of control, it moves into panic and we become helpless. Read the description below of someone who has climbed up a ladder and is now in a panic.

He looked up and heaved. He felt for the first time panicked beyond desperation, wildly violently loose. He almost let go. His senses screamed to let go, yet his hands refused to open. He was stretched on a rack made by these hands that would not unlock their grip and by the panic desire to drop. The nerves left his hands so that they might have been dried bones of fingers gripped round the rungs, hooks of bone fixed perhaps strongly enough to cling on, or perhaps at some moment of pressure to uncurl their vertebrae and straighten to drop. His insteps pricked with cold cramp. The sweat sickened him. His loins seemed to empty themselves. His trousers ran wet. He shivered, grew giddy, and flung himself frog-like on the ladder.

William Sanson

1 ☆ Notice the use of short sentences for effect. Changing the length of sentences can be a useful device when you are writing to create a sudden dramatic feeling. In the following passage someone is walking home and thinks they are being followed. Rewrite it using some very short sentences to make the writing more effective. Make any other alterations which you think would improve the piece.

The footsteps had been behind her for some time so she stopped, turned around and looked down the dark alley.

She could not see anyone and thinking, perhaps, she had made a mistake, she carried on walking, this time going a little faster.

The footsteps started again and now she had a good idea that someone was following her. Her heart started to beat faster and she quickened her pace as she turned onto the street where she hoped to see other people.

The street was empty with not a soul in sight. She started to run and could hardly believe it when the footsteps behind her also broke into a faster pace. She didn't dare look round but ran as fast as she could, fumbling for her key as she went.

She reached her front door, turned the key in the lock, threw herself inside, slammed the door and burst out crying.

2 Write a paragraph of your own in which you describe being out at night and think you are being followed. Plan your paragraph before you write it. Try to make it lead up to a climax like the one above. Include these four - or more - stages.

- Stage 1   Slight nervousness brought on by something.
- Stage 2   You might hear something, without being sure what it is.
- Stage 3   Something else happens to increase your fears.
- Stage 4   You give in to your fears in some way.

FEAR IN THE HOME

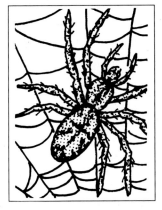

Are you terrified of snakes? Does the sight of a spider reduce you to jelly?

When the fear of something becomes so intense that people's lives are affected, it is called a phobia. It is thought that about one person in 30 - more than a million and a half people - in Britain have phobias.

It is easy to understand a fear of, say, snakes, but there are more than 300 named phobias and some of them are very strange. Can you understand terror caused by... seeing a beard, being touched, a piece of string? Yet these are all identified and named phobias. They are called, respectively, pogonophobia, haphephobia and linonophobia. You name it and someone may have an irrational fear of it. Tchaikovsky, the composer, was worried for many years in case his head fell off.

Some people's phobias are comparatively common and may seem understandable. You might know someone who is frightened of enclosed spaces, or water, or a particular animal. But these may be normal fears. It is not a phobia until it becomes so overwhelming the person is reduced to helplessness.

You may dislike spiders. But an arachnophobic (a person with a spider phobia) will feel panic and may be overcome by sickness, dizziness or burst into tears at the sight of one. To reason with them that a spider is harmless has no effect. An arachnophobic will avoid all places where there is a danger that a spider might be present. That is pretty nearly everywhere, and shows just how intolerable life can be if you have a phobia. There are, for example, people who for many years have refused to go out of their houses on their own because they are frightened by open spaces.

Can anything be done to help phobics? It can if the phobic wants to be cured enough. The most common treatment is something called "Behavioural Therapy". The idea is that the person suffering from the phobia is gradually introduced to whatever it is that they fear until they can cope with it. Imagine a man has a phobia about mice. A first stage could be for him to watch a mouse through a glass window, then be in a room where a mouse is in a cage and, step by step, move towards the time when he could let a mouse run over his hand. This process could take many months with lots of stages, each one representing a small advance. It could only work if the man really wanted to be cured.

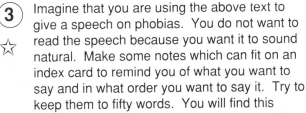

Now try . . . . . .

3 Imagine that you are using the above text to give a speech on phobias. You do not want to read the speech because you want it to sound natural. Make some notes which can fit on an index card to remind you of what you want to say and in what order you want to say it. Try to keep them to fifty words. You will find this exercise useful when you have to give a talk to the class.

4 Work out a possible course of Behavioural Therapy treatment for someone who has a phobia about moths. Include as many stages as you can - at least twelve. Remember, every stage should be only a very small advance or your step-by-step approach will break down.

5 Which phobia goes with which meaning in the table below? Check your answers by using a dictionary. Which language does each word come from? (Answers on page 96.)

PHOBIA	MEANING
Claustrophobia	fear of birds
Agoraphobia	fear of snakes
Bibliophobia	fear of pleasure
Clinophobia	fear of standing up
Hydrophobia	fear of insects
Necrophobia	fear of speaking
Stasiphobia	fear of water
Ornithophobia	fear of death
Ophidiophobia	fear of enclosed spaces
Halophobia	fear of books
Entomophobia	fear of open spaces
Hedonophobia	fear of going to bed

3.3 Fear as Control.

Throughout history and still today some governments use fear as a form of control. Can you think of any other situations in which fear is used in this way?

At the beginning of the novel *Great Expectations* by Charles Dickens, the young Pip is suddenly startled in the churchyard cemetery. Notice the five points indicated in the story.

H old your noise!'' cried a terrible voice, as a man started up from among the graves at the side of the church porch.

"Keep still, you little devil, or I'll slit your throat!"

A fearful man, all in coarse grey, with a great iron on his leg. A man with no hat, and with broken shoes, and with an old rag tied round his head. A man who had been soaked in water, and smothered in mud, and lamed by stones, and cut by flints, and stung by nettles, and torn by briars; who limped and shivered, and glared and growled; and whose teeth chattered in his head as he seized me by the chin.

"O! Don't cut my throat, sir," I pleaded in terror. "Pray don't do it, sir."

"Tell us your name!" said the man. "Quick!"

"Pip, sir."

"Once more," said the man, staring at me. "Give it mouth!"

"Pip, Pip, sir."

"Show us where you live," said the man. "Pint out the place!"

I pointed to where our village lay, on the flat in-shore among the alder trees and pollards, a mile or more from the church.

☞ The man, after looking at me for a moment, turned me upside down, and emptied my pockets. There was nothing in them but a piece of bread. When the church came to itself - for he was so sudden and strong that he made it go head over heels before me, and I saw the steeple under my feet - when the church came to itself, I say, I was seated on a high tombstone, trembling, while he ate the bread ravenously.

"Now lookee here!" said the man. "Where's your mother?"

"There, sir!" said I.

☞ He started, made a short run, and stopped and looked over his shoulder.

"There, sir!" I timidly explained. "Also Georgiana. That's my mother."

"Oh!" said he, coming back. "And is that your father alonger your mother?"

"Yes, sir," said I. "Him too, late of this parish."

☞ Ha!" he muttered then, considering. "Who d'ye live with - supposin' you're kindly let to live, which I han't made up my mind about?"

"My sister, sir - Mrs Joe Gargery - wife of Joe Gargery, the blacksmith, sir."

☞ "Blacksmith, eh?" said he. And looked down at his leg.

After darkly looking at his leg and at me several times, he came closer to my tombstone, took me by both arms, and tilted me back as far as he could hold me; so that his eyes looked most powerfully down into mine, and mine looked most helplessly into his.

"Now lookee here," he said, "the question being whether you're to be let to live. You know what a file is?"

"Yes, sir."

"And you know what wittles is?"

"Yes, sir."

After each question he tilted me over a little more, so as to give me a greater sense of helplessness and danger.

"You get me a file." He tilted me again. "And you get me wittles."

He tilted me again. "You bring 'em both to me." He tilted me again.

"Or I'll have your heart and liver out." He tilted me again.

He gave me a most tremendous dip and roll, so that the church jumped over its own weather-cock. Then, he held me by the arms in an upright position on the top of the stone, and went on in these fearful terms: 'You bring me, tomorrow morning early, that file and them wittles. You bring the lot to me, at that old

Battery over yonder. You do it, and you never dare to say a word or dare to make a sign concerning your having seen such a person as me, or any person sumever, and you shall be let to live. You fail, or you go from my words in any partickler, no matter how small it is, and your heart and your liver shall be tore out roasted and ate. Now, I ain't alone, as you may think I am. There's a young man hid with me, in comparison with which young man I am a Angel. A boy may lock his door, may be warm in bed, may tuck himself up, may draw the clothes over his head, may think himself comfortable and safe, but that young man will softly creep and creep his way to him and tear him open. I am a keeping that young man from harming of you at the present moment, with great difficulty. I find it wery hard to hold that young man off of your inside. Now what do you say?" I said that I would get him the file, and I would get him what broken bits of food I could, and I would come to him at the Battery early in the morning.

"Saay, Lord strike you dead if you don't!" said the man.

I said so, and he took me down.

"Now," he pursued, "you remember what you've undertook, and you remember that young man, and you get home!"

"Goo-good night, sir, " I faltered.

☛ "Much of that!" said he, glancing about him over the cold wet flat. "I wish I was a frog. Or a eel!"

At the same time, he hugged his shuddering body in both his arms, clasping himself, as if to hold himself together - and limped towards the low church wall. As I saw him go, picking his way among the nettles, and among the brambles that bound the green mounds, he looked in my young eyes as if he were eluding the hands of the dead people, stretching up cautiously out of their graves, to get a twist upon his ankle and pull him in.

When he came to the low church wall, he got over it, like a man whose legs were numbed and stiff, and then turned round to look for me. When I saw him turning, I set my face towards home, and made the best use of my legs.

On the edge of the river I could faintly make out the only two black things in all the prospect that seemed to be standing upright; one of these was the beacon by which sailors steered - like an unhooped cask upon a pole - an ugly thing when you were near it; the other a gibbet, with some chains hanging to it, which had once held a pirate. The man was limping on towards this latter, as if he were the pirate come to life, and come down, and going back to hook himself up again.

(1) The writer tells the story from Pip's point of view. Pip is the *Viewpoint Character*. He can only describe what he sees but we as readers may understand much more. At each of the five points indicated, Pip does not know what the strange man is thinking but we can guess.
  ● If this were drawn in cartoon form, the author might have put in thought bubbles to show us what the man is thinking at these points.
  ● Working in pairs, decide what you imagine he might be thinking and write five appropriate thought bubbles.

(2) This passage captures Pip's fear but it also contains humour. From Pip's point of view the incident is frightening, from ours it is amusing. Which parts do you think are amusing?

(3) In telling the story from the point of view of Pip, the author sometimes repeats sentences and phrases. Where and why?

(4) The man invents a non-existent character to terrify Pip even more. Look at the precise details of this character. Adults sometimes use fantasy creatures to try and frighten young children into doing what they are told. Either remember one such creature from your past or invent one. Write a paragraph using the creature as a threat.

(5) Do you think it is right that adults use fantasy in this way?

3.4 Enjoying Fear.

The title of this section may sound odd but if you think about it almost everyone enjoys putting themselves in situations in which they are afraid as long as it is controlled.

(1) Locked in a haunted house? Falling into a snake pit? What sorts of frightening situations can you think of? How many such situations have you been in? List them and share the stories with the rest of the class.

(2) When you watch a frightening film, it is not so much the climax of the action which is scary but the slow build up, the music, the use of close-ups, expressions on people's faces. The two scenes here are from a storyboard for a film showing the beginning of the scene and the climax. Create the tension by filling in the intervening scenes. Make a rough sketch and give a brief explanation for each new scene.

Do people enjoy hearing ghost stories? They certainly have a fascination whether we believe in them or not. The poem below captures that mixture in interest, excitement and fear.

I Like to Stay Up

I like to stay up
and listen
when big people talking
 jumbie stories

Oooooooooooooooooh
I does feel so tingly
and excited
inside - eeeeeeeeee

But when my mother say
"Girl, time for bed"
Then is when
I does feel a dread
Then is when
I does jump into me bed
Then is when
I does cover up
from me feet to me head

Then is when
I does wish
I didn't listen
to no stupid jumbie story
Then is when
I does wish
I did read me book instead.

Grace Nichols

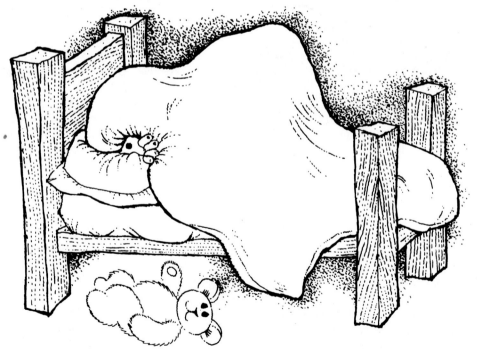

(3) First read the poem aloud and then write the poem out in Standard English. Compare the two. You will probably find that you have
☆ completely destroyed the poem! Sometimes it is appropriate to use Standard English but other times as in the case of this poem dialect is more appropriate. Why?

Tom Colley's Ghost

In 1751, near the town of Tring in England, an old couple were beaten and drowned by a frenzied mob who thought they were witches. The leader of the mob, Tom Colley, was later arrested and sentenced to death by hanging. When he was dead, his body was suspended from the gallows inside a gibbet - a cage of iron hoops and chains. It was left to dangle there as a gruesome warning to other lawbreakers. People believed that a person's spirit could not leave the Earth to go to the afterlife - heaven or hell - without a burial ceremony. So Colley's ghost would haunt the spot where he was left to rot. Other ghosts were thought to be the spirits of people who had been murdered or who had died very suddenly.

Colley's body, in its gibbet, was suspended at a crossroads. It was thought that his ghost would be confused by all the roads. Therefore it would not be able to find its way back to take revenge on the people who had hanged him there. His ghost is still said to haunt the place of the hanging. Recent stories say that his ghost now appears as a large black dog.

④ This ghost story is presented here in written form. Originally it would have been passed on by word of mouth. In pairs, one person should read the story twice, put down the book and then retell the story orally - perhaps using a tape-recorder. The other person should note down any points about the spoken version which make it different from the written version. Can you see how stories get changed when they are passed on orally? Have you noticed anything about how spoken language is different in many ways from written language?

⑤ Choose a situation which you think would frighten you. This is your title. Look back at the notes you made about fear (page 21). Write either a paragraph or a free verse poem which re-lives the situation.

Now try . . . . . .

6 ☆ The following activity shows you one way to plan a story, which you might like to use in an adapted form with other stories during the year. Do not hurry over it.

- ✓ In pairs decide on a crisis in which someone is overcome by extreme fear. Write it down in outline.
- ✓ Think of as many possible reaons for this crisis as you can and write these down using just one sentence for each.
- ✓ Do the same for the outcomes.
- ✓ Consider the variety of combinations by matching possible reasons and outcomes.
- ✓ Each of you can choose a different set of combinations and then write your story as effectively as you can. Concentrate on:
- ● making the reason believable
- ● making the crisis vivid
- ● making the outcome exciting and satisfying.

7 Prepare a radio documentary called "What Frightens You?" You could include interviews with people, investigative reports, stories like the one printed above.

4.1 Travel.

In this unit you will be focusing on practical and imaginative aspects of travel. You will also be using language to describe, report, argue and explain.

You might find it useful to discuss the following questions in groups of two or three before writing your responses. The cartoons represent common methods of travel.

1 Write down as many advantages and disadvantages for each of the four forms of travel as you can think of. Set the results out in a comparison table.

2 Can you think of circumstances in which one of the methods of transport here might be preferable to the others? Try it for each in turn.

3 In general, which form of transport do you prefer and why?

4 Which form of transport is better for the environment? Give your reasons.

Now try . . . . . .

5 You are a minister making a bid for extra funding from the government to be spent on developing the road, airport or rail network in the country. Prepare a five minute speech which you will deliver to the class, designed to persuade them that your bid is the most worthy.

6 Prepare a television advertising campaign to persuade people to use trains rather than cars.
☆
- At whom will the advertisements will be targeted?
- During which programmes will they run?
- How many advertisements will you use?
- What aspects of the transport will you stress?
- Design the advertisements in the form of story boards with commentary.

Train services Durham - London - Durham

Mondays to Saturdays

	Durham depart	Darlington depart	Kings Cross arrive
x	0603	0621	0859
⊘	0623b	0641b	0935
x	0630c	0650c	0950
⊘	0658	0716	1033
P	0705sx	0724sx	0955
	0705so	0724so	1000
⊘	0748	0806	1054
x	0848	0906	1150
x	0948	1006	1254
		1033	1308
⊘	1048	1106	1350
x	1148	1206	1448
⊘	1230so	1248so	1552
	1248sx	1306sx	1553
⊘	1316so	1335so	1652
	1348sx	1406sx	1655
		1432sx	1705
x	1454so	1513so	1825
⊘	1514sx	1533sx	1811
		1632sx	1911
x	1648sx	1706sx	1954
⊘	1654so	1713so	2025
		1730sx	2008
x	1759e	1835sx	2119
⊘	1902so	1920so	2232
x	1917sx	1935sx	2222
⊘	1957so	2015so	0050
⊘	2017sx	2036sx	2321

INTERCITY

Notes

SO	Saturdays only
SX	Saturdays excepted
b	Change trains at Doncaster.
c	Change trains at Northallerton.
e	Runs Mondays to Fridays. Change trains at Darlington.
f	Change trains at Darlington.
g	Change trains at York.
P	InterCity Pullman (except Saturdays and Bank Holidays) with full meal service to First Class ticket holders in designated seats. Buffet service of hot food, sandwiches, hot and cold drinks available to all passengers Mondays to Saturdays. Facilities available for whole or part of journey.
x	Full meal service (restricted to First Class ticket holders in designated seats on some trains) Mondays to Fridays. Buffet service of hot food, sandwiches, hot and cold drinks available to all passengers Mondays to Saturdays. Facilities available for whole or part of journey
⊘	Buffet service of hot food, sandwiches, hot and cold drinks available to all passengers. Facilities available for whole or part of journey.

Times in **bold** type indicate a direct service.
Times in light type indicate a connecting service.

Mondays to Saturdays

	Kings Cross depart	Darlington arrive	Durham arrive
⊘	0605	0908	0928
⊘	0650	0949b	1009b
x	0730sx	1015	1035
⊘	0730so	1019	1039
x	0800sx	1035	
⊘	0800so	1041	
⊘	0900sx	1136	
⊘	0900so	1138	1210c
x	0930	1214	1210c
x	1000sx	1232	1235
⊘	1030so	1255	
x	1100sx	1332	
⊘	1100so	1339	1422c
x	1130sx	1411	1359
⊘	1230sx	1511	1431
⊘	1230so	1522	1531
x	1300		1542
⊘		1600e	1622e
⊘	1330fo	1617	1637
⊘	1400sx	1627	
⊘	1400so	1648	1708
⊘	1430sx	1715	1736
⊘	1500sx	1727	
⊘	1500so	1805e	1814c
⊘	1530sx	1814	1825e
x	1530so	1826	1835
x	1600sx	1827	1846
x	1630sx	1919	1903c
x	1700sx	1930	
⊘	1700so	1944	1950
			2004
P	1730sx	2002	2022
x	1800sx	2036	2152c
⊘	1800so	2053	2113
⊘	1814fo	2058	2118
x	1900sx	2138	2158
⊘	1900so	2153	2213
⊘	1950so	2312	2332
⊘	2000sx	2237	2257
⊘	2040fo	2322	2343
⊘	2200sx	0037	0059
	2200so	0248	0308

7 You have to travel from Durham to London leaving on the Friday morning and arriving no later than 2.00 p.m. You have to return on Saturday and be back by 4.00 p.m.
- Plan your journey using the timetables shown here.
- What facilities can you expect on the trains you will be using?
- Will you need to change trains?

(handwritten letter)

24, Fieldhouse Lane,
Durham.

Dear Sir,
Last week I went on a journey. The train arrived very late and the train was extremely dirty. When I got off the train in London when it eventually arrived I went complain to the manager but he was very rude. That is no way to treat customers. I was late for my appointment and it was not convenient

Yours sincerely,
emma

8 Several problems arose on the journey and you decided to write a letter of complaint. Printed below is your first draft. The repetition of some words sounds awkward and you have failed to give precise details. As it stands, this letter will achieve nothing.
- Decide what you want your letter to achieve and then rewrite it as effectively as you can.
- Exchange letters with a friend and discuss whether the rewritten letters would cause anything to happen about your complaint.

Now try . . . . . .

9 You will need to do some research for this project. The telephone book might be a useful starting point. Write a leaflet of one side of paper, (folded in three) designed to give visitors to your area a guide to the main forms of transport. You will need to give details of the main bus and train stations, airport and taxi ranks.

Below is a leaflet which describes three possible routes for a road which will by-pass a residential area of a city. The leaflet has been designed in order to consult the views of the public.

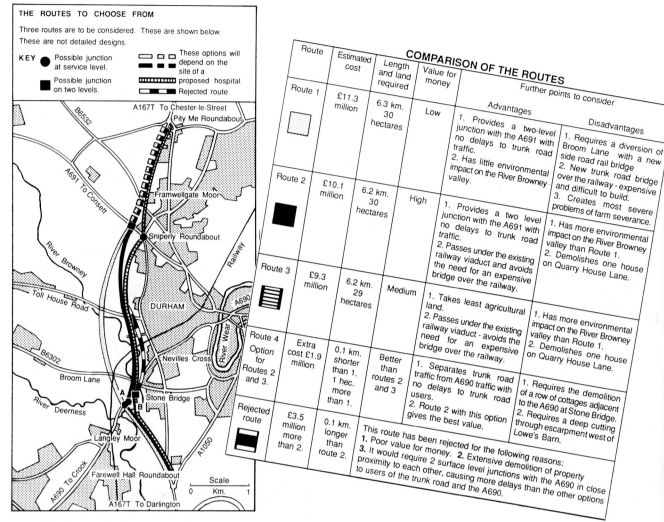

THE ROUTES TO CHOOSE FROM

Three routes are to be considered. These are shown below. These are not detailed designs.

KEY
- ● Possible junction at service level.
- ■ Possible junction on two levels.
- ▭ ▭ ▭ These options will depend on the site of a proposed hospital.
- ▬▬▬ Rejected route.

COMPARISON OF THE ROUTES

Further points to consider

Route	Estimated cost	Length and land required	Value for money	Advantages	Disadvantages
Route 1	£11.3 million	6.3 km. 30 hectares	Low	1. Provides a two-level junction with the A691 with no delays to trunk road traffic. 2. Has little environmental impact on the River Browney valley.	1. Requires a diversion of Broom Lane with a new side road rail bridge 2. New trunk road bridge over the railway - expensive and difficult to build. 3. Creates most severe problems of farm severance.
Route 2	£10.1 million	6.2 km. 30 hectares	High	1. Provides a two level junction with the A691 with no delays to trunk road traffic. 2. Passes under the existing railway viaduct and avoids the need for an expensive bridge over the railway.	1. Has more environmental impact on the River Browney valley than Route 1. 2. Demolishes one house on Quarry House Lane.
Route 3	£9.3 million	6.2 km. 29 hectares	Medium	1. Takes least agricultural land. 2. Passes under the existing railway viaduct - avoids the need for an expensive bridge over the railway.	1. Has more environmental impact on the River Browney valley than Route 1. 2. Demolishes one house on Quarry House Lane.
Route 4 Option for Routes 2 and 3.	Extra cost £1.9 million	0.1 km. shorter than 1. 1 hec. more than 1.	Better than routes 2 and 3	1. Separates trunk road traffic from A690 traffic with no delays to trunk road users. 2. Route 2 with this option gives the best value.	1. Requires the demolition of a row of cottages adjacent to the A690 at Stone Bridge. 2. Requires a deep cutting through escarpment west of Lowe's Barn.
Rejected route	£3.5 million more than 2.	0.1 km. longer than route 2.	This route has been rejected for the following reasons: 1. Poor value for money. 2. Extensive demolition of property 3. It would require 2 surface level junctions with the A690 in close proximity to each other, causing more delays than the other options to users of the trunk road and the A690.		

(Map locations shown: A167T To Chester-le-Street, Pity Me Roundabout, B6532, A691 To Consett, Framwellgate Moor, Sniperly Roundabout, Railway, River Browney, Toll House Road, DURHAM, A690, River Wear, B6302, Nevilles Cross, Broom Lane, River Deerness, A1050, Stone Bridge, Langley Moor, A690 To Crook, Farewell Hall Roundabout, A167T To Darlington, Scale 0 Km. 1)

(1) List the general points the leaflet is asking the public to consider when making their decision.

(2) Who will gain most by the construction of the by-pass? Who has most to lose?

(3) Which of the three routes would you choose and why?

(4) Prepare a questionnaire to be distributed with this leaflet, designed to get maximum information from the public on their views.

(5) The leaflet does not say why a by-pass is needed. Write a short statement to accompany the leaflet giving the reasons which you think are behind the plan.

(6) ☆ Draw your own plan of a town with a proposed by-pass drawn in. You can base it on where you live or it can be entirely made up. Role play a public meeting called to hear people's views on the by-pass.

(7) You are a newspaper reporter who has been sent to get a "human interest" story to go with the factual account in the paper.
Some ideas:
- details of an old person whose house might be knocked down;
- details of accidents which have happened on the existing road;
- interviews with people who live on the route.
Write the newspaper article.

Today people travel for a variety of purposes but not usually in the hope of discovering new countries and new people. Many years ago travellers' books were very common, often containing very tall stories. Here is an example from the sixteenth century.

And in those isles are many manners of folk of divers conditions. In one of them is a manner of folk of great stature, as they were giants, horrible and foul to the sight; and they have but one eye, and that is in the midst the forehead. They eat raw flesh and raw fish. In another isle are foul men of figure without heads, and they have in either shoulder one, and their mouths are round shaped like a horseshoe, y-midst their breasts. In another isle are men without heads; and their eyes and their mouths are behind in their shoulders. In another isle is manner of folk that has a flat face, without nose or eyes; but they have two small holes instead of eyes, and they have a plat mouth, lipless. In another isle are foul men that have the overlip so great that, when they sleep in the sun, they cover all the visage with that lip.

In another isle are folk whose ears are so syde that they hang down to the knees. Yet is there another isle where the folk have but a foot, and that foot is so broad that it will cover all the body and ombre it from the sun. And upon this foot will they run so fast that it is (a wonder) to see. Also there is another isle where the folk live all with the savour of a manner of apple; and if they tharned that savour, alsone they should die. Many other manner of folk there are in other isles thereabouts which were too long to tell all. For to go from isles by sea toward the east many days journeys men find a great kingdom, the which is called Mancy.

From this land men shall go to the land of Bachary, where are many wicked men and fell. In this land are trees that bear wool, as it were of sheep, of which they make cloth. In this land also are many ypotams, that dwell some time upon land and some time on the water; and they are half man and half horse. And they eat men whereso they may get them, no meat gladlier. And in that land are many griffins, more than in any country else. And some men say that they have the shape of an eagle before, and behind the shape of a lion and sickerly they say sooth. Nevertheless the griffin is more and stronger than eight lions of these countries, and greater and stalworther than a hundred eagles.

Sir John Mandeville

(8) List words in the passage which we no longer use today. Can you guess what they mean from the context?

(9) Rewrite pararaph two of the passage in clear, modern English.

(10) This passage contains grammatical constructions which are no longer used - the word order in some of the sentences is not what we would expect to read today.
☆
● Find examples and describe how the word order is different.
● You will need to use terms like *adjective, verb, noun, subject, predicate*.

Now try . . . . . .

11 Write your own traveller's tale, making it as far-fetched as you wish.

In the following story, a young girl goes on a train journey by herself.

Sitting opposite Nazreen in the railway carriage were two young children. The girl of about four or five was carefully crayoning a picture in a large colouring book. The boy was a little younger and had nothing to do; he clearly felt left out of things. Without warning he picked up a bright red crayon, leaned over, and scrawled it over his sister's picture. After that, things happened quickly. The girl screamed and hit out wildly, catching her brother full in the face. He started to bawl and grabbed her hair. By now arms and legs were flying in all directions and just as Nazreen was wondering if she was going to be caught up in it, the children's mother returned from the toilet.

"Now, what's this all about?"

"Sam started it ..."

"Julie hit me ..."

"He spoiled my picture ..."

"My nose hurts ..."

It took a full five minutes of Mother's soothing voice before calm was restored. Julie began working on another picture, and Sam had a sheet of paper of his own and was happily filling it with vivid colours. Only then could Mother return to her seat across the gangway.

Nazreen watched all this from behind her magazine. She wasn't really reading the magazine but it stopped people trying to talk to her. She was 12 years old and had no younger brothers or sisters.

This train journey promised to be entertaining. It was the first time she had travelled on a train by herself, and she had been rather nervous about the prospect even though her aunt had promised to meet her at the other end.

It didn't take long before Sam tired of crayoning. He reached over to grab Julie's book and for a moment it looked as though mayhem was about to break out again.

"Can I see your picture, Sam?" Without thinking, Nazreen had stepped into the fray, startling herself in the process. Was this really Nazreen speaking, the shy Nazreen that she and all her friends were used to? Anyway, it was in the nick of time. Julie's scream froze on her lips and Sam was shocked into stillness, his arm still stretched out.

"What have you drawn?"

"It's Benson."

"It doesn't look anything like Benson," said Julie scornfully.

"Yes it does."

"Who's Benson?" asked Nazreen.

"He's our dog," said Julie, "but he doesn't look anything like that."

Before Sam could reply their mother stood up. "I'm just going to the buffet to get us all something to eat. Be good while I'm gone."

She disappeared out of the carriage.

Nazreen felt apprehensive. They were in the last carriage and it was nearly empty. The only other people were at the far end, and seemed to be asleep. In effect she had been left in charge. Without thinking what she was doing she put her magazine down and took the initiative.

"I can see it's a dog, now." Sam looked pleased but Julie glowered. "Can I see your picture, too?" Nazreen asked Julie, but Julie wasn't going to be nice to any friend of Sam. She pulled her picture away, and at that moment there was a sudden sharp jolt and grinding of brakes. As the train decelerated Nazreen was thrown across the table. The two children had their backs to the engine, so they were just pushed against their seats, but a plastic bag fell from the rack above and showered them both with apples, sweets and biscuits. They started to scream.

"Don't cry. We're all right. We'll soon clear this away," said Nazreen rather desperately, but words were not going to calm the two frightened children. Nazreen had no time to be frightened herself. As the train slowed down, she stood up, ignoring her bruises, and went round the table to clear up the mess. Immediately, Sam grabbed her and when Julie saw this she threw herself across Sam towards Nazreen. Another fight was imminent. Quickly, Nazreen sat down between them amid the chaos, and to her surprise the two children snuggled up to her, whimpering. Well, she thought, one problem at a time. At least they were quiet. The mess could wait. She sat there without moving, an arm around each child. Gradually the whimpering stopped and deep breathing took its place. The two children had fallen asleep. This was not what Nazreen had anticipated and she tried to extract herself, but every time she moved one or other of the children moaned and snuggled closer. She was trapped.

Time passed. Just what had happened to their mother, Nazreen wondered. She should have been back ages ago. The guard approached, hurrying down the coach.

"Er, excuse me," began Nazreen, but he rushed past with a quick, "Can't stop now."

A few minutes later there came a message over the intercom. "If there is a Mr Salisbury on the train, please would he make his way to the Buffet Car where his wife has met with a minor accident."

Nazreen listened vaguely but she was more concerned with her own plight. She was helpless. She was also uncomfortable - her right arm was going to sleep. She waggled her fingers furiously and tried to think. They were going to arrive in Birmingham in about half an hour.

That was her stop. She hadn't much time. She must go and look for the mother. But she couldn't leave the children. There was only one thing for it. They would have to come with her.

Carefully she took hold of Julie's shoulder and began to shiggle her into wakefulness. Julie's eyes opened slowly and stared uncomprehending at Nazreen.

"Hello Julie. All right now?"

Julie's face started to crumple. "Where's my Mam?"

"Now Julie, listen carefully. Don't cry. Everything's all right. We are going to walk down the train to your mother." Nazreen was careful not to suggest that they had actually lost her! "Help me to waken Sam."

That was more difficult. Sam was fast asleep and would not waken up. In the end Nazreen had to carry him and so she set off down the train with Sam clinging round her neck and Julie holding tightly on to her spare hand.

Just as they set off the train braked again, more gently this time. Over the intercom came the voice of the guard once more.

"We are making an emergency stop at Burton-on-Trent station. We apologise to passengers for any inconvenience caused by the delay."

Nazreen and the children were about halfway down the train when it stopped. Farther down the platform Nazreen could see a crowd of people. Some, in uniform, were standing by a stretcher on wheels.

Then two men climbed carefully out of the carriage, carrying someone wrapped in a blanket. They placed the patient on the stretcher. The train door slammed, a whistle blew, and the train began to move.

What happened next lasted only a few seconds, but it seemed like a nightmare to Nazreen. As they passed the stretcher it was being turned round on the platform. For an instant the patient's face was turned towards Nazreen at a distance of about ten feet. There was no mistaking who it was - the children's mother. Instinctively Nazreen called out, "Please - stop the train. Quickly. Help, someone."

The passengers around her looked embarrassed. No one moved at first. Then someone came towards her talking in soothing tones. But no one was doing anything to help and the station platform was slipping past. Nazreen was becoming desperate.

Then, suddenly, she remembered her father joking about what he had called the "Communication Cord", but which he said was now a red handle on 125 trains. "Don't pull that whatever you do," he had said, "or it'll be the end of your pocket money for this year!"

Nazreen dropped Julie's hand ignoring her scream of protest, plonked the sleeping Sam on to the lap of a surprised lady, jumped on to a seat and pulled on the red handle as hard as she could.

Once again the train braked sharply, but this time it wasn't going very fast so the shock was less.

Within seconds the carriage was full of hubbub and confused action. Everyone was talking at once. Julie was screaming. Only Sam was silent - sleeping peacefully, his thumb in his mouth. The guard arrived and took charge. When he heard what Nazreen had to say, his angry expression changed.

"Oh, I see. Well, just come along with me. Bring the children and we'll soon sort this out. Their mother didn't seem to be badly hurt but she was unconscious. She hit her head when the train braked suddenly some way back. She's on the way to hospital for a check-up."

It didn't take long to collect the luggage and an official took the children off the train. They weren't sorry to leave Nazreen despite clinging to her earlier. To be honest, Nazreen wasn't sorry to see them go. They had caused her enough trouble for one day.

The train arrived in Birmingham thirty-five minutes late.

Nazreen put on her coat and lifted her case down from the rack. She stood up and turned to leave. Then she remembered her magazine, moved to pick it up, and stopped. "I don't really want that any more," she thought, and left it lying on the table as she went to meet her aunt.

(1) What do you think would make a good title?

(2) It is not necessary for a reader to know how long the events described in a story would actually take but it can be a useful way of looking at a story again more closely. Try to work out what the time-span is from the start to the end of the story to the exact minute. You may find differences of opinion in the class.

(3) Notice that the author only gives us the detail necessary for the story to work. It is not necessary for us to know why the characters are going on the journey but it can be interesting for us to speculate.
  ● Why might the mother and children be taking this journey?
  ● Why might Nazreen have been going to her aunt?

(4) Imagine that after the events of the story the mother is writing to a friend explaining what happened from her point of view. Remember that you will have to invent some details not in the story and you will have to decide how much the mother would learn about what happened in the carriage when she was gone. Write the letter she sent.

(5) At the end of the story Nazreen leaves her magazine behind. This is a small detail but it is essential to the whole story.
  ● Why does the author include that detail?
  ● Look for two other references to the magazine at the start of the story and part way through.

(6) A pupil who read this story said that Nazreen could be described as having a journey in more ways than one. What was meant by that statement?

Now try . . . . .

7 Some writers use the idea of a journey as a symbol for a journey through life.
  ● Draw a diagram which represents your life so far in the form of a journey, showing high and low spots. Use the idea of going up and down mountains, along a train track through tunnels or anything else you can think of.

8 Have you ever been sitting in a train carriage sitting opposite people and tried to guess something about them? It can pass the time away! Appearance gives your first clue, followed by anything they are carrying. If they speak that might help also.

9 Write your own story based on a train journey.
☆
  ● You could begin as follows: "Sitting opposite me in the railway carriage was/were..."
  ● Or you might prefer to write in the third rather than the first person in which case you could begin, "Sitting opposite ...." and insert the name of a character.

SEE FOR YOURSELF

TRAVEL AT THE SPEED OF

SOUND

CHANCE OF A LIFETIME

Only

$45

Eurodollars

VISIT THE PLANET

ZARG

VIEW THE EXTRAORDINARY LIFE FORMS

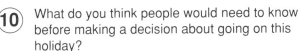

10 What do you think people would need to know before making a decision about going on this holiday?
- Write a letter to the company which organised the holiday, asking the questions to which you want answers.
- You might want to know about the climate, the cost of things and so on.

11 Write the text for the courier (the travel company's representative whose task it is to look after the people on holiday) as people board the spaceship.

12 In pairs, imagine one of you has just returned from the travel experience, and the other is interviewing him or her for a travel programme.

Now try . . . . . .

13 Create your own advertisement for a travel holiday, but set it EITHER in the past OR in the future. The advertisement here is one set in the future: an advertisement for people to join a pilgrimage in the time of Chaucer is an example of one set in the past. Make sure you get your facts right.

In this unit you will be working in groups of between four and six people. Each group will produce a single copy of a magazine.

You will work through a series of six tasks as follows:

- Task 1   Overall planning.

- Task 2   Drafts.

- Task 3   Editing.

- Task 4   Content decisions.

- Task 5   Publication copies.

- Task 6   Synthesis.

☆ **TASK 1. Overall planning.**

Elect an editor who will make decisions in case of disagreement.

MALE FASHION
FEMALE FASHION
CHILDREN'S FASHION

CONTROVERSIAL MATTERS
YOU MUST BE FAIR!
GIVE BOTH SIDES OF THE ARGUMENT

RECORD REVIEW
FILM REVIEW
BOOK REVIEW
TV REVIEW

INTERVIEW
CURRENT AFFAIRS
SCHOOL NEWS

SPORTS REPORT
HOBBIES
CLUB/SOCIETY NEWS

SHORT STORIES
POEMS

SAFETY IN THE HOME
HOME MAINTENANCE
RECIPES
HOME FURNISHING IDEAS

QUIZ
JOKES/CARTOONS
ADVERTISEMENTS

BIRTHDAY ANNOUNCEMENTS
GOSSIP COLUMN
LETTERS TO THE EDITOR
PROBLEM PAGE
HOROSCOPES

Choose at least ONE article from at least SIX of the nine sections listed above.

Allocate articles among group members. The editor should keep an overall list of who is doing what.

TASK 2. Drafts.

Work on your contribution(s). Think carefully about who is going to read your work - who is going to be your audience? Will this influence the way the work is produced? At this stage do not worry too much about how it looks; your contribution will be edited by another member of your group. Make a draft, as accurately as you can, but knowing it will be improved later.

DO YOU NEED *Illustrations?*
• Drawings? WHERE?
• Magazine pictures? WHERE?
• COLOUR!! WHERE?

 ## TASK 3. Editing.

Pass your work on to another member of the group for editing. This task will be even easier if you have used a word-processor! In turn, you will edit someone else's work. In this way, everyone's piece of work will be edited by someone else in the group and then passed back to the author with comments.

When you are editing someone else's work, ask yourself the following questions:

Did I enjoy it?
Are there parts which could be improved?
Can I suggest any additions?
Do I recommend publication or rejection?

Then pass the work back with any written suggestions for improvements.

TASK 4. Content decisions.

You need to decide together about the following:
Which pieces will be included? There must be at least one from each member of the group.
What is to be the design of the cover and who is to do it?
What is to be the order of the contents and who will produce a contents page listing them?
Is the magazine going to be printed in some way or hand-written?

You will also have to consider the overall look of the magazine...

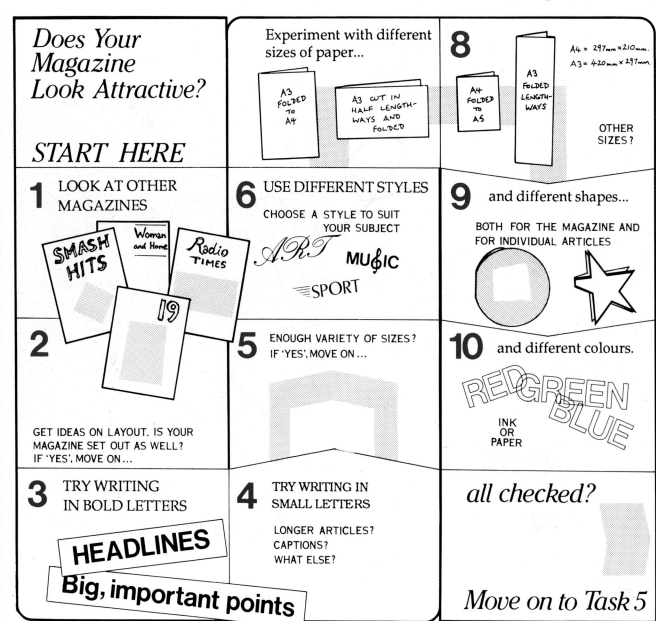

Does Your Magazine Look Attractive?

START HERE

Experiment with different sizes of paper...

A3 FOLDED TO A4

A3 CUT IN HALF LENGTH-WAYS AND FOLDED

8

A4 FOLDED TO A5

A3 FOLDED LENGTH-WAYS

A4 = 297mm × 210mm.
A3 = 420mm × 297mm.

OTHER SIZES?

1 LOOK AT OTHER MAGAZINES

SMASH HITS

Woman and Home

Radio TIMES

19

6 USE DIFFERENT STYLES

CHOOSE A STYLE TO SUIT YOUR SUBJECT

ART   MUSIC

SPORT

9 and different shapes...

BOTH FOR THE MAGAZINE AND FOR INDIVIDUAL ARTICLES

2

GET IDEAS ON LAYOUT. IS YOUR MAGAZINE SET OUT AS WELL? IF 'YES', MOVE ON...

5 ENOUGH VARIETY OF SIZES? IF 'YES', MOVE ON...

10 and different colours.

RED GREEN BLUE

INK OR PAPER

3 TRY WRITING IN BOLD LETTERS

HEADLINES

Big, important points

4 TRY WRITING IN SMALL LETTERS

LONGER ARTICLES?
CAPTIONS?
WHAT ELSE?

all checked?

Move on to Task 5

TASK 5. Publication copies.

Now you need to make final copies of your contributions, having agreed on how your particular contributions are to look, and taking into account any suggestion for improvement.

When you have finished you will need to proofread it very carefully so that there are no mistakes. It is sometimes easier to spot other people's mistakes, so it is best to do this in pairs, proofreading each other's work.

CHECK LIST
Check that
☆ your magazine cover gives sufficient information
☆ all contributors are acknowledged
☆ the contents page is complete
☆ pages are numbered.

O.K. Ed.
What do you think?

IS IT....	Eye catching?	Easy to follow?
	YOU MUST READ THIS !!	CONTINUED ON PAGE 11, THEN PAGE 6 AND THERE'S A LITTLE BIT ON PAGE 2
Too overcrowded?	Too much blank space?	Illustrated so it looks more interesting?
	NEWS / A BIT MORE NEWS	NEWTON DISCOVERS GRAVITY!
Colourful?	Subtitled?	Clearly written, typed or word-processed?
FREE SUNGLASSES (YOU'LL NEED THEM!)	A BORING STORY - THE GRIPPING TALE OF LIFE IN THE TEXAN OILFIELDS!	

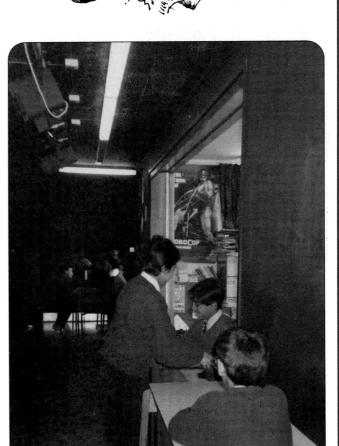

TASK 6. Synthesis.

Now you need to put the magazine together and add any finishing touches to make it more inviting and interesting to your reader. Who will read it outside your classroom? Invite people to the launch of your magazine. Where will this be held? Whom will you invite?

In this unit you will be thinking about the ways certain things change over time, particularly language. You will also be giving attention to the use of verbs in your writing.

A

Lor! I've tried for thirty years and can't get one!

B

I want to see the place where the noise comes from.

C

Hallo! Is that Scotland Yard? This is Susie Smiff. Have you seen my kitten?

D

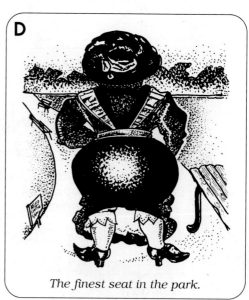

The finest seat in the park.

1 In pairs look at the cartoons above. They are obviously from the past. How can you tell? Discuss the objects drawn, the styles of dress, the language used, the type of drawings and the nature of the humour.

2 Make 2 columns headed PAST and PRESENT. In one column list as many details from the pictures which indicate a bygone age. In the other list what we might expect instead, today.

3 Has humour changed over time? Consider the cartoons shown here, old films you may have seen and any other evidence you can think of.

4 Sometimes writers think up cartoons but give detailed instructions for an artist to draw their idea. Choose one of the cartoons here and write out detailed instructions for an artist so that the cartoon can be drawn exactly. Swop what you have written with a partner so that the accuracy of your instructions can be checked.

These are extracts from the School Rules of Kingswood School, a boarding school which John Wesley founded in the middle of the eighteenth century.

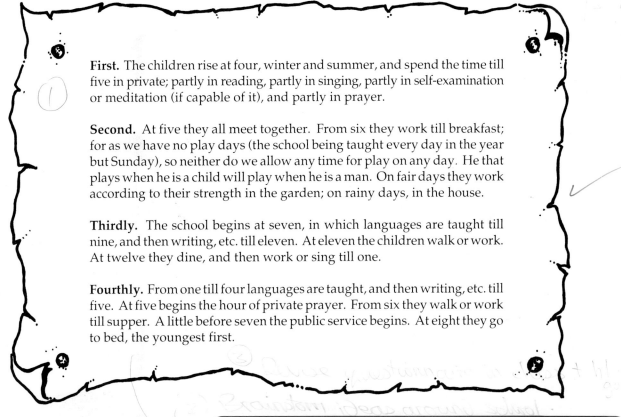

First. The children rise at four, winter and summer, and spend the time till five in private; partly in reading, partly in singing, partly in self-examination or meditation (if capable of it), and partly in prayer.

Second. At five they all meet together. From six they work till breakfast; for as we have no play days (the school being taught every day in the year but Sunday), so neither do we allow any time for play on any day. He that plays when he is a child will play when he is a man. On fair days they work according to their strength in the garden; on rainy days, in the house.

Thirdly. The school begins at seven, in which languages are taught till nine, and then writing, etc. till eleven. At eleven the children walk or work. At twelve they dine, and then work or sing till one.

Fourthly. From one till four languages are taught, and then writing, etc. till five. At five begins the hour of private prayer. From six they walk or work till supper. A little before seven the public service begins. At eight they go to bed, the youngest first.

Now try . . . . . .

5   How have schools changed over the years? Ask older people to find out.

6   Look at your own school rules. Imagine that you have the opportunity to cancel one of the rules and put a new one in its place. Decide which one you wish to get rid of and which new rule you wish to make, and prepare your case. Make notes so that you can deliver a short speech to the rest of the class to argue your case. The class could listen to six speeches and vote on which change sounds most convincing.

7
☆   Develop a class project on changing times. In small groups decide what aspect of the theme "changing times" you are going to work on for a class display. Agree on a subject which allows everybody in the class to develop some aspect they are interested in. Ideas:
● changing styles in cars
● the way your local area has changed over the years
● changing attitudes to entertainment
● changes brought about by computers
● changes in what people wear
● changing lives of teenagers.

6.2 Changing Language.

Read this passage. You will find it much easier than it first seems.

The blonke was maily, like all the others. Unlike the others, however, it had spiss crinet completely covering its fairney cloots and concealing, just below one of them, a small wam.

It was quite drumly - lennow, almost samded in fact. When yerden it did not winx like the other blonkes or even flerk. The other blonkes, which had not been given the same nesh, were by no means lennow or samded. They winxed readily enough.

The nesh was quite kexy, had a strong shawk, and was probably venenated. There was only one thing to do with it - gevel in the wong and gaff it in. This would be much better than to sparple it in the flosh as the blonkes that were not drumly could iswonk in the wong but not in the flosh. And in any case, it might not be wise to venenate the flosh.

1 Can you answer the following?
- Where was the small *wam*?
- What is *drumly*?
- Why were the other *blonkes* not *lennow* and *samded*?
- In what way was the *drumly blonke* like/unlike the others?
- If *nesh* is *venenated*, is it wise to *gaff* it in the *wong*?

2 Did you find you were able to answer the questions, even though you did not understand every word? You should have been able to answer every question correctly. Why is that?

In fact the words here are not nonsense words but they are all English words which are now obsolete - they are not in common usage now. Here is what some of the words mean:

Blonke = small white horse
Maily = speckled
spiss = matted
crinet = hair

cloots = hoof
yerden = to hit with a stick
nesh = food

Can you now guess what some of the others mean? If you can, it is because you have more information about the CONTEXT. It is often possible to guess the meaning of words when you look at them in context, that is in relation to other words in a passage or sentence.

Now try . . . . . .

3 Although the words in the passage were used at one time, you would not have found a passage written exactly like this at the time the words were used. Can you think of a reason why that is the case?

4 Make up three sentences each containing one nonsense word. Do so in such a way that it is not impossible to guess what the word might mean. Swop with a partner and see if you can guess the meanings from the context.

Language of course changes over time. But it does not just change in terms of the words we use but also in terms of grammar. Can you match the following extracts to the costumes and in turn to the dates? Be careful - one of the dates and costumes cannot be matched! (Answers on page 96.)

A

Hir coverchiefs ful fine weren of ground;
I dorste swere they weyeden ten pound
That on a Sonday weren upon hir heed.
Hir hosen weren of fyn scarlet reed,
Ful streite yteyd, and shoes ful moiste and newe.
Boold was hir face, and fair, and reed of hewe.

(a)

C

I was ever of opinion that the honest man, who married and brought up a large family, did more service than he who continued single, and only talked of population. From this motive, I had scarcely taken orders a year, before I began to think seriously of matrimony, and chose my wife, as she did her wedding gown, not for a fine glossy surface, but such qualities as would wear well. To do her justice, she was a good-natured, notable woman; and as for breeding, there were few country ladies who could show more. She could read any English book without much spelling; but for pickling, preserving, and cookery, none could excel her. She prided herself also upon being an excellent contriver in housekeeping, though I could never find that we grew richer with all her contrivance. However, we loved each other tenderly, and our fondness increased as we grew old.

(c)

B

It was Miss Murdstone who was arrived, and a gloomy-looking lady she was; dark, like her brother, whom she greatly resembled in face and voice; and with very heavy eyebrows, nearly meeting over her large nose, as if, being disabled by the wrongs of her sex from wearing whiskers, she had carried them to that account. She brought with her, two uncompromising hard black boxes, with her initials on the lids in hard brass nails. When she paid the coachman she took her money out of a hard steel purse, and she kept the purse in a very jail of a bag which hung upon her arm by heavy chains, and shut up like a bite. I had never, at that time, seen such a metallic lady altogether as Miss Murdstone was.

(b)

(d)

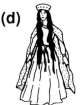

D

Her fat old red face with its parrot beak nose in the middle of it, her little plump hands, her figure as well filled as a church rat's, her full and flabby bust harmonise with the room which sweats misery, where enterprise is blotted out of life; whose cold and noisome atmosphere Madame Vouquer yet can breathe without being made sick. Her face, fresh as the first frost of autumn, her wrinkled eyes, the expression of which has a range from the ballet dancer's smile to the bill discounter's malignant scowl, her whole person illustrate the boarding-house, just as the boarding-house implies the mistress. The prison and the warder go together, you cannot conceive one without the other.

(5) Do the changing costumes tell you anything about the changing role of women through the ages?

(6) Each of the four extracts gives a description of a woman. What can you deduce from each passage about the way the women described in each passage lived and dressed? Do you have any opinions about the role expected of women?

(7) What changes in the language can you detect? List words which you do not understand. List any sentences which have a word order which we would not expect to find today.

Robert Westall

I was painting me seven-hundreth railing. In wi' the scraper, ripping off the faded blue flakes, scattering them like flowers on the sick January grass. Again I heard the echo of Granda's voice.

"If you're doing owt, son, mek a job of it."

Granda even made a job of dying. Torpedoed twice in the War, but Jerry couldn't kill him. Fell off a ladder at the age of seventy nine, painting his own guttering. A stroke, the doctor said. Dead before he hit the ground. Christ I miss him.

I eased me muscles, looked back along all the railings I'd done, stretching down the hill. Glad they were bright orange, brave against the grey January sky, the grey works, grey steam billowing from grey chimneys. Making a lot of steam the works was, but not much chemical. Hardly a feller in sight. Rationalisation, they said, redeployment. Ha bloody ha. That works had been the town's Big Mammie for a hundred years. Fat pay-packets and all the copper wire you could nick, smuggled out wrapped round your belly under your shirt.

Big Mammie's sick, maybe dying. Keep on painting the railings; stops you going bonkers.

Six months back, when we'd just left school and were rotting on the dole, they'd really conned us wi' Job Creation. Moving into the realm of new technology, gaffer said first morning, his spectacles winking shifty under the neon-lights. How to live at peace wi' the computer! Chance of a real job at the end, if you showed the makings!

We really lapped it up, that first morning, in our shining-bright safety-helmets. Overalls so new they argued back as you walked. First lunchtime we swaggered down to the shops wearing the lot; clattering our boots 'til we drove the old granny in the off licence mad. We are the ICI boys!

Once, I even got a chance to help a fitter wi' a faulty pump. And a fitter is what I want to be. The pump was a small, shiny, beautiful piece of craftsmanship. I put my head close to it an' listened, like Granda used to. Which noise was the fault? The thin tapping at the top, or the wheezing like bronchitis in the round, curly middle?

"What yer reckon?" I asked the fitter. That's how fitters talk to each other.

"What yer mean, what yer reckon?" He had a little sneaky putting-down grin on his face.

"What's up wi' pump?"

"Aah don't give two damns. It's coming out, that's all Aah know."

He cut the power wi' a red button; turned a yellow wheel to cut off the flow of chemical. Started undoing the pump's screws. One stuck. He took a hammer to it. The shining metal dented, crumpled, collapsed in a wreck. Bloody German rubbish," said the fitter, pulling the wrecked pump free and throwing it on a trolley. "Get that packing case open, kid, will ya?

Wi'out breaking what's inside, right?"

Inside was another pump exactly the same.

"Why didn't we mend the old one?"

"Cheaper to buy new. Pumps is cheaper than fitters."

"Me Granda..."

"Your Granda went down wi' the Titanic, kid! This is today."

"Call yerself a fitter?" I shouldn't ha' said it; but he shouldn't ha' said that about Granda. He thought about clouting me one, then noticed me size. He kicked the pump instead, like it was a dead cat, and wheeled it away.

The next week, the pound started climbing against the dollar. The Americans stopped buying chemicals. The works started making steam instead. The bosses started walking round like they were going to their own funeral, and we were all put on painting railings. There were eight of us, wi' a foreman, painting railings round a wood next the works. Within a week, Bowlby began pissing about, snapping the thin branches off the chemically poisoned trees and throwing them in the soupy yellow river. The foreman caught him an' played hell. Bowlby just laughed an' went right on doing it. Soon all the rest were doing it, an' the foreman didn't come round much any more, except wi' the packets on payday.

I tried larkin' about wi' them once; but it made me feel like a little kid, so I jacked it in. There's point in going backwards. But they went on wi' it. I'd see them through the trees, lighting fires, roasting stolen taties, toasting sandwiches, like chimpanzees in safety-helmets. Sometimes they shouted I was licking the foreman's arse, but I ignored them and they soon got tired.

I was halfway down my seven-hundred-an'-first railing when I heard the noise they were making change; their voices went quieter, a creepy sort of gloating. I tried to ignore it, but I knew they were going to hurt something. Something worse than trees. Not me, mind. I'm big, and when I land somebody one...

Finally, I couldn't bear it. I stuck me brush back in the paint and walked towards their sodding fire. One or two of them saw me, and ran ahead through the trees, shouting I was coming. Bowlby had a cat; a poor thin white thing; from the look on his face, he wasn't thinking of feeding it sandwiches. He had a bit o' rope round its neck. It had its ears back, terrified but still hopeful. It licked his hand.

So it was me an' Bowlby again. It always was. The rest o' the kids were nowt, shadows hanging round the edges.

"What you doing wi' cat?"

"None of your business."

"I'll mek it my business," I looked round the rest.

They kept their eyes down. One had a brick in his hand. So they were going to drown the cat. Coulda' been worse. Bowlby'd roast the cat alive ...

"I'll tek that cat."

Bowlby watched me coming. I began to think that the poor cat was the cheese in the trap; an' I was the poor bloody mouse.

"C'mon, mek me," said Bowlby. I'd have been scared, but for his eyes. They were rovin' all over the place, half cocky, half doubtful. Telegraphing Granda called it.

I moved in on him. I tell you, I was pig-sick wi' six months o' painting railings. Just lookin' for something to smash that needed smashing. Like Bowlby. But I was scared of hurting the cat.

He threw it in my face. A good trick, but for his telegraph-eyes. And I don't play goalie for nowt. I had that poor cat snatched lefthanded against my chest and still had time to see Bowlby's kick coming. I grabbed his foot and just held it there, giving it the odd twist for good luck. Then I pushed the foot up an' back.

He kept his feet, just. At the cost of running backwards about fifteen feet like something out of Laurel and Hardy. Trouble was it carried him back to the steep, slippery river-bank, and down he went in a slather of foam, like a depth charge exploding in the Yellow Sea.

I laughed myself sick; a shit like Bowlby where he belonged at last. Just in time, I realized nobody else was laughing. Next second, they were all on me. I'd never have thought they had it in them. But they meant it, boots an' all.

I managed. I had to punch one-handed, wi' the cat. But I stood back an' punched big - a couple o' golden handshakes they won't forget. But they just stood back then, an' started throwing things.

I turned me back on them, and walked off through the wood. One stone rattled on me helmet, but they didn't follow. Maybe they were givin' Bowlby the kiss o' life.

I kept walking, blind wi' misery. It wasn't just me bruises; it was suddenly knowing how much they hated me, how they'd planned the whole thing. And the bloody railings, and even that was coming to an end and then it'd be the dole again an' lying in bed 'til children's telly started, trying to think of some reason for getting up. Even school would've been better. And I'd left me flask and sandwiches back there. An' Mam wouldn't let me take the cat home an' the stupid thing would go back to the wood an' the next time they'd do it in for sure. I just hated the whole of bloody 1982 and wished to hell I was somewhere else, anywhere ...

So, I never really grasped how I got out o' the far side o' the wood and into that slum. Never seen a slum like it. They were so poor they couldn't even afford telly; not an aerial in sight. The houses were the usual Coronation Street, but they'd made no efforts, not even a lick o' paint. The streets were cobbles; the gutters full o' dirty soapy water an' little kids were playing in them wi' matchbox boats, wi' a match for a mast an' a little bit o' paper for a sail. They got up an' stared at me open-mouthed as I walked past. They had big boots an' maroon jerseys that buttoned at the neck an' skin-head hair cuts and trousers that hardly covered their knees. Stared at me like I was a Martian, snot hanging from their noses that they wiped on the cuffs o' their jumpers, and great big shadowed eyes. I felt embarrassed, a bit. I suppose I did look funny, walking along wearing a safety-helmet an' carrying a cat. But I hung on to the cat. I had a feeling that if I let go, it wasn't long for this world. It was thin as razor blades, and shivering in great convulsive shivers. Nothing that a month of home cooking wouldn't cure but ...

Where was home? I hadn't a clue. Never been down this part of town in my life. The street-name said "Back Brannen St". Never heard of it. There were four men on the corner, squatting on their haunches, wearing caps, looking like Norman Wisdom multiplied by four.

"Excuse me," I said, staring down at them.

"Yes kidder?" asked one, kindly.

"I've got meself a bit lost."

"Ye're a bit big for that. Where'd ye want, kidder?"

"I live on the Marden Estate," I said stiffly.

"Marden Estate? Never heard of it . Hev ye Jackie?"

Another man shook his head. "Aah've heard of

Sea-Coal.

Lord Redescapes' Estate, and Sir Percy Hambly's Estate. Never heard of Marden Estate. Heard of Marden Farm mind - very good place for sheep, is Marden Farm. D'you like roast mutton kidder?'' They all laughed, like there was a private joke they weren't letting on about.

''Marden Farm's near us,'' I said, ''except it was demolished 'afore I was born. We still got Marden Farm Road.''

''Demolished?'' asked the first man. ''That's a staff-officer's word for ye, Jackie! Last thing Aah saw demolished was a German strongpoint in Thiepville Wood.'' He brought a worn tobacco-tin out of his pocket, and took out a squashed flat dog-end. With loving care he pressed it back into shape. The tobacco inside rustled dryly. Then he took a pin from his coat-lapel, stuck it through the dog-end and lit up, turning his head carefully sideways, so he didn't burn his nose. He took one drag, and passed it to his mate. I watched as they solemnly passed it round the circle, like an Indian pipe of peace. Holding it by the pin; it had burnt down to quarter of an inch long, too small to hold between their fingers.

''D'you wanna fag?'' I burst out, horribly embarrassed. Took twenty king-size from my overalls and flipped it open.

They stared. ''Jesus God!'' said one. They didn't move. Just stared at the packet of twenty like they'd never seen one before. I grabbed five out of the packet and thrust them into the first man's hand, where it lay on his crouching knees.

He looked at me. ''Who are ye, hinny? Carnegie?''

It was all so strange, I ran.

As I turned the corner, I heard their mocking voices, calling like birds.

''Thank you, Carnegie.''

But round the corner was worse. A man sat on a doorstep, propped against the door. A fat man with no legs. Instead, he had big round black leather straps fastened round his waist. His fat face lifted, as he heard me running. His eyes were covered with small round dark glasses.

''Buy a box of matches, mate?''

I wanted to go on running, but a kind of nosy horror took me up to him. There was a flimsy wooden tray hanging round his neck by a piece of white tape. On it were nine boxes of matches. On the front of the tray was written DISABLED - THREE CHILDREN. There was a greasy cap on the pavement beside him, guarded by an old black dog, nearly as fat as the man.

''Help a wounded soldier, mate!'' he said, in a sing-song voice like a worn gramophone record ''Wife and three kids. Military Medal and bar.'' He pointed to the breast of his cut-down blue coat. There were four faded medal ribbons and a silver badge. His whole face strained towards me, through the round spectacles. ''Help an Old Contemptible, mate, what caught it at Wipers!''

I reached desperately into my overalls, and tossed two ten-pence pieces into his cap. His face frowned at the double clink. He scrabbled for the coins, felt their milled edges; bit them. Then he said,

''Two florins. God bless you, mate.'' I turned to go, but his big, warm hand reached out and clasped mine. ''Don't forget your box of matches, mate. And give us a hand up - it's me dinner-time.'' Suddenly he had both big hands on my shoulders, and was heaving himself upright onto the black leather pads. I had to brace my free hand between the wall to stop myself being pulled over on top of him. His breath, his warmth, the smell of his overcoat, were like a farm-animal's.

''Thanks, mate.'' He released me, and reached down for his cap, steadying his tray of matches with the practised hand. How could he be practised at having no legs? How could he exist, and even think of dinner, with no legs?

Unbearable. I ran, the safety-helmet bouncing like a pan on my head, the cat digging its claws into me, clinging on tight.

''You forgot your matches, mate!'' I looked back; he was following me, walking slowly on his leather pads, matchbox held aloft.

I ran up a side-alley. And another, and another. I ran a long time. When I came to myself, the alley had turned into a cinder-track between allotments. The allotments had funny high fences, made of the rough bark off pine-trees, cut into weird, wriggly shapes, full of knot-holes. There was a dripping tap, fastened to a wooden post, quite alone on a corner. Dripping gently on the cinders. I suddenly felt very thirsty; my mouth felt like a desert of alkali.

I was still guzzling when I heard a voice say, ''You'd better leave a bit of water for the plants.'' I looked up, dribbling water from my mouth over the cat's fur. Expecting another monster.

But he wasn't a monster. He was young - a bit older than me. Thin, but in a ruddy faced, fit sort of way. Bright, blue, friendly eyes, and a big ginger moustache, neatly trimmed. The only weird thing about him was his clothes - a battered suit with waistcoat and watch-and-chain. No collar an' tie, only a spotless white muffler. His cap, another Norman Wisdom special, was pushed back on his ginger curls, and he was leaning over his allotment gate, smoking a pipe. The thin blue smoke curled up in the calm air, and he looked totally contented. It was just funny, him being dressed like an old-age pensioner, and yet looking so young.

"Cat could do wi' a square meal," he said. "Why not give it an Oxo cube?"

"Just rescued it," I said. "Some kids were goin' to drown it."

"Got a few scraps." He opened his gate, as slowly and grandly as if he was the Duke of Newcastle.

Mind you, even the Duke of Newcastle wouldn't have minded owning what was inside. A long path of old brick stretched into the distance, through three trellis archways hung wi' pink roses. The well-raked soil bulged with healthy-looking flowers, better than my dad ever managed; all in well-drilled rows like soldiers on parade. There was a pigeon-cree, painted in green and white stripes, with ornate fretwork on top, full of plump cooing pigeons. Further on through the third trellis, vegetables. Turnips like cannon balls; cabbages like even bigger cannon balls. Hoed lines of potatoes. A tarred black hut, then a greenhouse full of thin-stemmed tomatoes, with yellow fruit.

My God, all this in January ... and that explained everything, the hollow-eyed kids, the man with no legs. I was dreaming.

Now I'm good wi' dreams, 'cos I dream a lot. And I've learnt to control them. If they start turning into a nightmare, I can wake up. But this dream, at the moment, was OK, so I let it be.

"We haven't been introduced," said the moustached guy, suddenly all stiff and formal. "Name's Billy Dack - put it there." He had a grip like a warm six-inch vice.

"Mike Anderton," I said, recovering my hand and flexing it behind my back, to restore the circulation. He fetched a crumpled packet of greaseproof paper, and began spilling out crusts and white pork-fat on the brick path for the cat. The cat lowered its tail, and ate with a desperate gulping motion.

"No breakfast," said Billy, "like three million others. You in work, then or still at school?"

"Job Creation," I said with grimace, "painting railings."

"You've not starved, though. Ye're a big lad for your age. Not shavin' get? Ye look fit enough for a

gentleman ... like to give me a hand?"

He pointed to a five-foot cylinder of rusting iron that stood by the greenhouse. All chimneys and levers and furnace-doors, like a little brother to Stephenson's Rocket.

"What the hell is it?" I asked.

He frowned, thunderously. "Watch yer language, son. Or I'll mek ye wash your mouth out wi' soap."

His blue eyes were very sharp; he looked like he thought he had the right to wash out my mouth with soap. Ah well, what did it matter in a dream?

"What is it?" I said, swallowing a sharp crack.

"It's an old donkey-boiler," he said, "off a ship. I'm fitting it into the greenhouse, to keep it warm, come winter."

"I'll give you a hand," I said. We struggled it into the greenhouse, and connected it to the hot-water system somehow, even though the two things clearly weren't meant for each other. He dragged out what he called his box o' bits - lead piping, old brass taps, great hanks of wire, old tin-openers, screws and nuts - a whole packing-case full. I watched him heat bits of metal red-hot in the stove of his hut, and hammer them into shape like a blacksmith.

"Are you a blacksmith?"

"Shipyard-fitter," he said. "'Til they sacked me, the minute Aah finished me apprenticeship. They're building ships wi' apprentices now, they can't afford to employ grown men."

We finished; he packed his box o' bits away. "Each bit o' that could tell his own story," he said.

"Never throw owt away, then ye'll never lack for owt. Well, Aah reckon ye've earned a bit o' bait. Kettle's on."

We went back to the hut. My, it was snug. Old black kettle singing on the stove. China cups and saucers wi' little rose-buds on them. Curtains at the window, and even a bunk wi' a patchwork quilt. He saw me looking at the bunk.

"Aah sleep here in the summer, for a bit o' peace and quiet. There's ten of us in three rooms, back home. Not room to swing a cat."

He looked into the teapot. It was half full of soggy tea-leaves. "Aye, I think that'll stand one more fill." When he poured the tea out, after a lot of stirring, it was as pale as lager; but he spooned two sugars into my cup without asking, and trailed in long strings of condensed milk from a sticky brown tin. It tasted great. Then he took down a tin with Japanese women painted all over it but most of them were worn away. He held it out to me.

It was full of stale, broken cakes. But he looked at me with the grand smile of a king, like he was giving me a real treat, so I took one.

"Aah load the bread carts for a baker every morning. Only takes an hour, and he gives me all of yesterday's leftovers. Keeps our family in bread an' cakes all week." He bit with gusto into a vicious coloured green triangle. My cake tasted like sawdust wi' pink icing, but he was watching so I ate it.

"Good, eh?" he said. "That's the best cake the baker does. You're a good chooser! And, bye the bye, what ye got yourself apprenticed as a painter for? From the way ye helped me wi' that boiler, ye'd make a canny fitter."

"I want to be a fitter," I spluttered, still battling wi' the sawdust.

"Then why don't you? Paintin's a softy's job. They're signing on apprentices at the North Eastern Marine - all they can lay their hands on. They'll sack ye at twenty-one, like they sacked me. but ye'd have a trade, an' things can't go on being bad forever."

"Me granda served his time at the North Eastern Marine. Goodwin Anderton he was called."

"Aah knew a Goodwin Anderton there," said Billy. "But he was an apprentice wi' me - a lad my age."

We stared at each other in growing silence. There just couldn't be two men called Goodwin Anderton - never in the history of the world ...

I took a deep breath and asked shakily, "What's the date, Billy?"

He reached for a pile of newspapers he kept handy for lighting the stove.

"Twenty-third of July - no, that's last Tuesday's - the twenty-sixth of July." The paper he was holding up was the Daily Mail. But it was twice the size it should be.

"What year?" I shouted.

"1932, of course."

"Oh, all right," I said to myself. "I'm dreaming and I don't like this dream any more. Wake up." I closed my eyes and willed myself to wake up as usual. All I got was a totally undreamlike pain on my shin. I opened my eyes to see him grinning and returning the steel-tipped toe of his boot under his chair.

"That wasn't part of no dream, bonnie-lad."

He didn't believe me about 1982 at first. But I had a newspaper, too, tucked into the pocket of me overalls. The Sun. He examined it with interest, until

he got to page three, then he stuffed it straight into the roaring stove.

"Ye mucky-minded little bugger!"

"Everybody reads it where I come from, even me Mam."

"You must have had a bloody funny bringing-up!"

I distracted him with my digital watch-calculator. Only I had a job to stop him taking the back off to see how it worked. I had to distract him again, wi' a king-sized fag. He lit up with gusto, using a burning piece of paper from the stove.

"Big as a toff's cigar!" He inhaled 'til the ends of his ginger moustache twitched.

"A toff like Carnegie?" I asked. He nodded.

"Who is Carnegie?"

"American. Biggest millionaire in the world, son. Lights his cigars wi' hundred-dollar bills." He sounded wistful, as if Carnegie lived in fairyland. And it was that wistfulness that brought it all home to me, that threw me in a panic.

"Billy - I'm caught. If I've travelled in time, how do I get back?" He eyed me coldly.

"Aah believe ye have. Like that feller in H.G. Wells - the Time Traveller. Come to think of it, you do look a bit like something out of H. G. Wells wi' that hat and that cat. Blimey - I'm a poet an' I don't know it!"

"But how do I get back?" I screeched.

"Aah'll bend me mind to it. Mind you, ye've no cause to grumble, even if ye can't get back. Ye've got a grand new pair o' boots there, that I bet don't let in water, and a watch anybody'd give a thousand pounds for, and enough spare flesh on ye to last three months. Come and help me gather sea-coal for the donkey-boiler, while Aah think about your dilemma."

I didn't notice much on our walk down to the sea; I was too worried. But there was a lot of horses and carts about; big piles of manure in every street. And kids running round in bare feet, though Billy said they preferred it that way in summer. I knew a lot of the houses, but there were gaps between, more green fields. And I saw a man with a wooden leg playing an accordian on the street corner.

The beach was just the same. And the castle on the cliffs. And the swimming pool, though it was brand-new concrete then ... the beach was cut in half, as if by a knife. The sunny, southern half was full of holidaymakers in deckchairs. A few, men and women, were wearing striped bathing-costumes that covered them nearly as much as clothes. But most people were sitting there in their Sunday best, hats an' all. There were three dignified men, grand wi' moustache and cap and watch-chain, paddling in the water up to their knees, and still looking like they were going to have a chat wi' King George the Vth. Somebody had a wind-up gramophone, and a whole crowd had gathered to listen.

The cold, northern end of the beach, shadowed by the cliffs, was nearly empty. Long black bands ran along it, round the high-tide mark. Sea-coal. Washed out of coal seams in the cliffs, by the waves. Washed off the decks of colliers in storms; washed out of wrecked ships over hundreds of years. I'd run across those black bands as a little lad, grumbled when they'd hurt my feet. Never realised what they were.

People here did. Well away from the holiday-makers, creeping like mice, frightened of being noticed and giving offence, crawled a grey stooping army of old women, thin coughing men and little kids. Each with their soaking black bag.

Between the sea-coalers and the holidaymakers, on the very edge of the sunlight, a policeman was standing, sweating in a serge collar done up to his neck.

"One of the toffs complains," said Billy, "he'll chuck us all off the beach. Aah wish ye'd left that bloody silly helmet behind. Ye're like something out of the Shape of Things to Come. Aah suppose Aah should be grateful you've left the bloody cat."

We got down to it. I followed him along one of the curving black bands, picking up tiny bits of coal. They were mostly smaller than peas. If you found one as big as a cherry, it was an event. You couldn't scoop them up in handfuls, or you just ended up wi' a sackful o' wet sand. You picked 'em one by one, like prize strawberries. If you bent down to pick 'em, your back hurt like hell. If you knelt, you got your knees soaked. I sort of went blind by the end, sweat dripping off me nose, just picking, picking. Billy left me far behind.

I carried me sea-coal home on me back. It dripped and made me bottom wet. We'd just got to the allotment gate when Billy said, "Here's poor Manly Gosling comin."

A ghost wavered down the cinder-track, a ghost so thin and staring-eyed that I hoped, I prayed, he'd walk straight past. But Billy said kindly, "What fettle the day, Manny?"

The ghost halted, swivelled his head. "Hallo, Marrer. Fair to middlin'." He pulled a spotless white hanky out of his pocket and began to cough into it. The coughing had a life of its own. The coughs grew bigger and bigger. Manny heaved and shook, as of some enormous, invisible animal had landed on his back and was tearing the life out of him. He clung to a fence post with his free hand, and the whole fence shook for twenty yards.

Then the white hanky blossomed a little pink rose. Another. Then a bigger red one. Then a whole bunch of roses. Blood and spit trickled down his spotless white muffler.

"Steady on, Manny," said Billy, gently, putting a strong brown hand over the thin pale hand that clutched the fence. It seemed to help. The coughing got less and less, and finally stopped.

"Better?"

"Better as Aah'll ever be, now."

"Come in for a cup of tea, Manny." And Billy opened the allotment gate as grandly as he'd opened it for me. But Manny wouldn't go into the hut with us.

"I'll stay out here, Billy. There's more fresh air out here."

"What's up wi' him?" I hissed.

"TB - consumption. He'll never see next spring. First cold east wind'll finish him."

"But we can cure TB easy. A few shots of penicillin - piece of cake."

"Aren't you the lucky ones?"

"But if I took him back to out time wi' me ..."

Billy gave me one of his sharp blue looks.

"You're very sure you're going back, all of a sudden. I thowt ye were stuck ..."

"I've been thinking ... if I just go back the way I came ... it's worth a try."

"Aye, it's that or nowt. Maybe you came on a return ticket, may be a single. There's only one way of finding out. But even if ye are on a return ticket, Aah reckon it'll be for one passenger, bonnie-lad. Nowt to do wi' me."

"I'd like you there, in case it doesn't work."

"Aye well we'll give Manny his tea, and take him an' all. He'd could do wi' a brave new world, could Manny."

We gave Manny his tea. I thought he was going to start coughing again, over the sawdust cake, but he managed to swallow it. He also managed to totter as far as Back Brannen St. The legless man was gone,

Sea-Coal.

thank God.

At the end of Back Brannen St was a pale blue railing, quite decently painted, with thin-leaved chemically-sick trees behind, that had a familiar look. Billy spoke to a couple of sunken-eyed kids who were playing with their matchboxes in the gutter. "Ye seen this feller before?" he said, pointing at me, all cat and safety-helmet again.

"Yes. He came out of that gate, but we couldn't get in - it's stuck now. It's always stuck."

I pushed the gate. The cat shivered. The gate opened easily. We passed through, all three of us.

Trod on through the silent, leafy, July trees. The air grew colder; the sky grew grey. Leaves seemed to be falling; at least the trees got more and more bare. Manny shivered, pulling up his jacket collar round his thin neck.

"Aah cannit go no further, Billy." He sank onto a fallen log. We stood around awkwardly. Ahead, I was sure I could hear crashing of branches, distant shouts. I thought I saw a glint of firelight through the winter trees; it was coming on dusk.

"C'mon, Manny," I said. "You must try. Not much further. There's doctors can make you well over there, Manny. Plenty o' food - nobody goes hungry."

"Sounds like the bleddy kingdom o' heaven," said Manny, and began coughing again.

I looked at Billy; he gave me a straight look back.

"I can't walk any further either, son. There's something holding us back." He nodded at the cat, held against my chest. "Reckon that's your return ticket son. I think I seen her over our side before. But she's only a ticket for one...."

I knew what he was thinking. If I let Manny hold the cat, Manny would go and I would stay.

"Aah know where Goodwin Anderton lives," said Billy. "He only lives three streets from us. Aah see him nearly every week ..."

I closed my eyes, and my head swam. Granda. Granda back. Granda young an' strong. A chance to do a real job; build ships instead of painting endless bloody railings. Hitler coming, and the War. Granda survived it, so could I. I hesitated.

Too long. Manny said, fretful, "Take us home, Billy. Aah'm catching me death o' cold, sitting here."

I looked at Billy again, but he was already hauling Manny to his feet.

"Tara, son," he said, wi' out looking at me. "Aah'll not tell Goodwin ye called - he's a mate o' mine!"

The way he said it, I'd rather he'd hit me.

They didn't seem to be walking very fast, but they vanished quickly amongst the trees, like smoke. At the same moment, the cat jumped out o' me arms and was off. By gum, I was scared then. I ran an' ran, until I was right among that lot at the fire.

"What's up wi' you?" asked Bowlby's mate. "You look like you seen a ghost." But Bowlby had knocked off early to get dry, and they weren't in a mood to try anything.

Then, of course, I had to go back; all the way to the gate that led onto Back Brannen St. Just to make sure I hadn't been dreaming after all.

The gate was still there; it needed painting, thick wi' rust. An' it didn't open when I pushed it.

Beyond? A bloody great open space, with drums of chemical piled under black polythene sheets. All the chemical the company couldn't sell to the Americans. Not a sign of Back Brannen St ...

It was all fading, just like a dream. I must've dreamed it all, I told meself, walking home.

Except when Mam made me take me dirty boots off, a little piece of coal fell out of them. No bigger than a pea ...

 1982 - 1932

☆ ● Life is grim in 1982 when the story opens. Life is also grim in 1932. Make a comparison of the good and the bad in 1982 and 1932 based on your reading of the story. You could set this out in columns or you might present your findings in the form of a display with illustrations.

● Do some research to find out about contrasting lifestyles in 1982 and 1932.

● When did you begin to suspect ... ? Mike realises what has happened to him when he sees the date on the copy of the Daily Mail. At what point did you suspect that Mike had travelled out of his own time? What are the clues that suggest this is the case?

2 LIFE IN 1982

Imagine you are an Environmental Inspector. You are concerned about waste, and the "Throwaway" society. Write a report for your Environmental Watch Group dealing with all the issues that concern you up until Mike enters the slum area.

3 MIKE, THE LONER

Mike is really one of a group of eight workers at ICI, painting the railings, but he ignores the rest. As a result, they gang up to persecute him. He seems to need to talk over what has happened with someone who will listen and help him to come to terms with it. Imagine that he was called into the office of a counsellor at ICI. In pairs role play the meeting which took place.

4 THE ENDING

Mike left 1932 and returned to the present. Why? Do you think he made up his own mind? What do you think Billy and Manny thought of him? What do you think Mike thought of himself? Don't just give an opinion - look for evidence in the story. Do you think Mike should have returned or stayed?

5 WHAT IF... ?

Many stories, like this one, are based on the premise, "What if?" The writer does not allow Mike to meet his grandfather as a young man. But what if he had? Write your account of their meeting. Or ... What if Mike had not hesitated, but given the cat to Manny before he had thought through what he was doing ? Continue the story.

☆ REMINDER - Verbs and Tenses.

There are more tenses than past, present and future, of course. Tenses enable us to say and write exactly what we mean. When your writing becomes complicated, you need to use, for example, the pluperfect tense - he HAD CLIMBED - or the conditional if he WERE TO CLIMB.

Consider the different shades of meaning in the following statements, all of which are in the past. How will the tone of voice change to reflect the different meanings?

I cleared up the mess I made.
I was clearing up the mess I made.
I did clear up the mess I made.
I have cleared up the mess I made.

Can you say *I was your friend* in different ways, changing the verb. Does the meaning change?

Now try . . . . . .

6
☆
Old people often enjoy talking about the past. You could prepare an interview with an old person so that you can either write down what they say or tape their conversation. Prepare the questions you will ask but do not turn the interview into an interrogation. Practise with a partner. When you have collected the interviews, report them or play them to the rest of the class.

7
☆
Have things changed much in your life? Things are changing all the time but we do not always realise it. Draw an autobiographical table, starting with the year you were born and going up to the present. List the main events in your life alongside main news events, changes in fashion, tastes in music, etc.

In this unit you will be reading and writing about the joys, advantages, problems and tensions of family living.

A

IDEAL HOME

GROOMED CLEAN HAIR.

SPARKLING TOOTHPASTE SMILE.

NEW CLEAN CAR

CLEAN PRESSED CLOTHES

WELL-KEPT GARDEN.

HEALTHY COAT.

In past ages members of a single family usually lived close to each other. So a child in those times would not only see her mother, father, sisters and brothers each day, but also her aunts, uncles, grandparents and cousins. That was called an extended family. Nowadays many different family groupings as well as the extended family are common. One is the much smaller unit where one or two parents live with maybe one or two children and have no relatives nearby. This is sometimes called the nuclear family.

Family life gives rise to all sorts of questions, the answers to which are very much a matter of opinion. You might find it useful to discuss these questions in pairs before giving your written views.

① When you think of the term "family" what image comes to mind? Figure A shows a humorous version of a typical image of a family as depicted in a television or magazine advertisement but of course advertisements rarely show what life is really like. List as many advertisements which include family scenes as you can think of. As you do so think about the type of family they are showing.

② Can you think of advantages and disadvantages of living in
a) a nuclear family
b) an extended family?
● What is the ideal size family in terms of numbers of children?
● Does the "only child" have any particular advantages/disadvantages?
● If a family adopts a young baby, at what age should they inform the child that it is adopted?
● Is it better for children from the same family to go to the same secondary school or are there advantages in going to different schools?

FOR ROLE PLAY

The following situations should raise a variety of questions about family life. If any group acts out the situation for the rest of the class, individuals can be asked questions while they stay in role.

(3) In pairs:

It is 11.30 p.m. The teenager was told to be in by 10.30 p.m. As he/she approaches the house it is all in darkness. What a relief! The key turns in the lock slowly and the teenager tiptoes into the hall. Suddenly a voice from the living room comes through the darkness. It is the parent who is waiting up! The conversation which follows has to take place in hushed voices in order not to wake up the rest of the household.

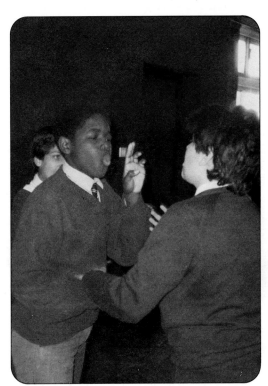

It is nearly the end of breakfast and time to leave for school. The second year pupil suddenly claims to be not feeling well. After much pressure, argument, coaxing, the parent eventually finds out the real reason why the pupil does not want to go to school today. The pupil should plan the reason without telling the parent before the start of the role play; try to make it original.

(4) In groups:

A family who has offered to give a young teenager a foster home is being interviewed by a social worker in their own home; the children of the family are present. It gradually becomes obvious that the family is not in full agreement and some of them are very much against the idea. You should decide who in the family is going to be hostile to the idea of having someone else join the family and let them work out their own reasons before the start of the role play.

A family are sitting at the living room table looking at brochures and trying to plan their summer holiday. One of the teenage children is not joining in very enthusiastically and it eventually comes out that he/she wants to go on holiday with friends this year. The rest of the family are not pleased. Before the start of the role play the family could work out the different reasons they have for not wanting the teenager to go on holiday with friends.

(5) Take one of these situations and extend it, or invent a situation of your own based on family life.

- Write it out in a script form for a radio play.
- Perform this to the class.
- Question the characters in the play in role about their attitudes and motives.

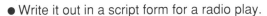
Now try . . . . . .

6 Write six days' entry of a diary in role kept by someone at a time when there was some tension or crisis in the family. It can be written from the point of view of any member of the family.

Adults in a small child's life are of supreme importance. Children are completely dependent on them. They are the source of all things, good or bad, so children soon learn to do what pleases those all-important people and brings the wanted rewards.

The baby girl who is pretty, who smiles sweetly at the father, who grips his finger clingingly, will be looked at lovingly by him, may be picked up and hugged. The baby boy who kicks his legs strongly, waves his hands around with great vigour, even cries loudly, equally delights his father, and brings forth approving noises and an extra hug.

The toddling boy who makes loud booming noises, who knocks things over, who pushes along a toy car with great vigour, who even gets his clothes dirty, will equally win his parent's approval. "Isn't he just like a little boy?" "A real little boy, isn't he?" "You can tell he's a boy can't you?" But what happens to the little girl who makes booming, zooming noises, or who stands on her head, or throws a ball hard across the room?

She is immediately aware she has done the wrong thing. Her father frowns, or pushes her away from him. Her mother or aunt or grandma is often equally critical. "That's too rough for little girls." "Little girls don't get their dresses dirty." "You must sit still and be a little lady." You don't believe me? Do an exercise in listening and studying. It is quite fascinating, once you start to notice, to find out how often exactly the same action from a little boy or a little girl will bring a completely different reaction from an adult.

Joyce Nicholson

1. In groups, read the passage and make sure you understand what the author is saying. It might be an idea to get one person to read it aloud.

2. Do you agree with the claim that young boys and girls are treated differently by their parents? What about when they get older?

3. ☆ What jobs are boys and girls expected to do in a family household? How are the jobs divided in your family?

4. Make a list of the toys which you were given when very young. Do boys and girls generally play with different toys? Do you think this makes a difference in later life?

5. "I personally do not believe it is any more 'natural' for all little girls to be passive and quiet, sweet and kind and clean, than it is 'natural' for all little boys to be aggressive and creative, competitive, tough and masterful, the boss." What do you think?

Now try . . . . . .

6. Collect advertisements from magazines which depict males, females or family groups and comment on the ways in which they are represented. For example, what sorts of jobs are the women shown performing?

7. Make two lists of what you would describe as typical comments made by adults to boys and girls. You could start by including the ones in the passage. How many can you add?

A class in an English lesson were set the tasking of writing a letter to someone which they know they would never actually have the courage to send. This was one of those letters.

? FJow
? MDMF

Dear Dad,

It may seem a bit odd for me to write you a letter when I see you every day but I will find it easier to put my thoughts into writing than actually talking to you. I do not want you to worry and start thinking that there is something terribly wrong – there isn't – but there are one or two things I want to say to you.

I am now thirteen years old and I would like to feel that I could be treated as someone of that age. Why do you make such a fuss over me wearing make-up? Virtually all the girls in my class do and their parents do not seem to mind. I can't really see what harm it does.

Neither can I see why you make such a fuss about the clothes I wear.

Surely it is natural for someone of my age to want to be in fashion again, it is hardly a crime or causing any harm to anyone.

However I do not want to dwell on make-up and clothes too much because that is not the real reason for this letter. Why is it Dad that you take such a delight in making fun of me all the time? I know you mean no harm and that you probably think you are being funny but it embarrasses me, particularly when my friends are around.

Last weekend when you came into the living room wearing my hat and ear-rings and "dancing" to the records I just wanted to die. My friends did not say much to me but I know what they were thinking. Even at breakfast time I can't open my mouth without you imitating what I am saying. It makes me feel like not talking at all.

I do not think I am badly treated. I know you probably mean well and care for me but the truth is that you are making me unhappy. When I read this letter everything I have put seems very trivial and silly. It is hard to explain why it is so important to me.

Much love

Lisa

Now try . . . . . .

8 Imagine that Lisa left this letter in her English file and it was found by her father. Write the reply he gave in the form of a letter.

9 Have you ever had any feelings similar to Lisa's? If so, describe what the circumstances were. Do you think she is being fair or unfair? Give your reasons.

10 Write an imaginary letter to someone (parent, friend, teacher) which the author of the letter would not actually have the courage to send.

The following story by Philippa Pearce describes an encounter between Joey and his great grandmother.

"Will my cousin Dicky be there?"

"Everyone's been asked. Cousins, aunts, uncles, great aunts, great uncles - the lot. It's your great grandmother's hundredth birthday party."

"But will Dicky Hutt be there?"

"I'm sure he will be."

"Anyway, Joe, why do you want to know?"

Joe's mother and father were staring at Joe; and Joe said, "I hate Dicky."

"Now Joe!" said his mother; and his father asked: "Why on earth do you hate Dicky?"

"I just do," said Joe. He turned away, to end the conversation; but inside his head was saying: "I'd like to kill Dicky Hutt. Before he tries to kill me."

When the day of the birthday came, everyone - just as Joe's mother had said - was there. Relations of all ages swarmed over the little house where great grandmother lived, looked after by Great Aunt Madge. Fortunately, great grandmother had been born in the summer, and now - a hundred years later - the sun shone warmly on her celebrations. Great Aunt Madge shooed everyone into the garden for the photograph. The grown-ups sat on chairs, or stood in rows, and the children sat cross-legged in a row in the very front. (At one end, Joe, at the other, Dicky; and Dicky's stare at Joe said: "If I catch you, I'll kill you ...") There was a gap in the centre of this front row for a table with the tiered birthday cake and its hundred candles.

And behind the cake sat great grandmother in her wheelchair, with one shawl over her knees and another round her shoulders. Great Aunt Madge stood just behind her.

Great grandmother faced the camera with a steady gaze from eyes that saw nothing by now - she had become blind in old age. Whether she heard much was doubtful. Certainly, she never spoke or turned her head even a fraction as if to listen.

After the photograph and the cutting of the cake, the grown-ups stood around drinking tea and talking. (Great grandmother had been wheeled off somewhere indoors for a rest.) The children, if they were very young, clung to their parents; the older ones sidled about aimlessly, except that Joe could see Dicky always sidling towards him, staring his hatred. So Joe sidled away and sidled away ...

"Children!" cried Great Aunt Madge. "What about a good old game? What about hide-and-seek? There's the garden to hide in, and most of the house."

Some of the children still clung to their parents; others said "Yes" to hide and seek. Dicky Hutt said "Yes". Joe said "No"; but his father said impatiently: "Don't be soft! Go off and play with the others."

Dicky Hutt shouted "I'll be He!" So he was. Dicky Hutt shut his eyes and began to count at once. When he had counted to a hundred, he would open his eyes and begin to search.

Joe knew whom he would search for with the bitterest thoroughness: himself.

Joe was afraid - too afraid to think well. He thought at first that he would hide in the garden, where there were at least grown-ups about - but then he didn't trust Dicky not to be secretly watching under his eyelashes, to see exactly where he went. Joe couldn't bear the thought of that.

So, after all, he went indoors to hide, but by then some of the best hiding places had been taken. And out in the garden Dicky Hutt was counting fast, shouting aloud his total at every count of ten. "Seventy!" he was shouting now; and Joe had just looked behind the sofa in the front room, and there was already someone hiding under the pile of visitors' coats - "Eighty!" came Dicky Hutt's voice from the garden - and two children already in the stair-cupboard, when he thought of that hiding place. So he must go on looking for somewhere - anywhere - to hide - and 'Ninety!' from outside - anywhere to hide - and for the second time he came to the door with the notice pinned to it that said: "Keep out! Signed: Madge."

"A hundred! I'm coming!" shouted Dicky Hutt. And Joe turned the handle of the forbidden door and slipped inside and shut the door behind him.

The room was very dim, because the curtains had been drawn close; and its quietness seemed empty.

But Joe's eyes began to be able to pick out the furnishings of the room, even in the half-light: table, chair, roll-top desk, and also - like just another piece of furniture, and just as immobile - great grandmother's wheelchair and great grandmother sitting in it.

He stood, she sat, both silent, still; and Dicky Hutt's thundering footsteps and voice were outside, passing the door and then far away.

He thought she did not know that he had come into her room; but a low, slow voice reached him: "Who's there?"

He whispered: "It's only me - Joe."

Silence; and then the low, slow voice again: "Who's there?"

He was moving towards her, to speak in her very ear, when she spoke a third time: "Who's there?"

And this time he heard in her voice that little tremble of fear: he recognised it. He came to her chair, and laid his hand on hers. For a second he felt her weakly pull away, and then she let his hand rest, but turned her own, so that his hand fell into hers. She held his hand, fingered it slowly. He wanted her to know that he meant her no harm; he wanted her to say: "This is a small hand, a child's hand. You are only a child, after all." But she did not speak again.

He stood there; she sat there; and the excited screams and laughter and running footsteps of hide-and-seek were very far away.

At last, Joe could tell from the sounds outside that the game of hide-and-seek was nearly over. He must be the last player not to be found and chased by Dicky Hutt. For now Dicky Hutt was wandering about, calling: "Come out, Joe! I know where you're hiding, Joe - I shall find you!"

The roving footsteps passed the forbidden doorway several times; but - no, this time they did not pass. Dicky Hutt had stopped outside.

The silence outside the door made Joe tremble: he tried to stop trembling, for the sake of the hand that held his, but he could not. He felt that old, old skin-and bony hand close on his, as if questioning what was happening, what was wrong.

But he had no voice to explain to her. He had no voice at all.

His eyes were on the knob of the door. Even through the gloom he could see that it was turning. Then the door was creeping open - not fast, but steadily; not far, but far enough.

It opened far enough for Dicky Hutt to slip through. He stood there, inside the dim room. Joe could see his bulk there: Dicky Hutt had always been bigger than he was; now he loomed huge. And he was staring directly at Joe.

Joe's whole body was shaking. He felt as if he were shaking to pieces. He wished that he could.

His great grandmother held his shaking hand to hers.

Dicky Hutt took a step forward into the room.

Joe had no hopes. He felt his great grandmother lean forward a little in her chair, tautening her grip on his hand as she did so. In her low, slow voice she was saying: "Who -" And Joe thought, He won't bother to answer her; he'll just come for me."

But the low, slow voice went on: "Whoooooooooooooooo -" She was hooting like some ghost-throated owl; and then the hooting raised itself into a thin, eerie wailing. Next, through the wailing, she began to gibber, with effect so startling - so horrifying - that Joe forgot Dicky Hutt for a moment, and turned to look at her. His great grandmother's mouth was partly open, and she was making her false teeth do a kind of devil's dance inside it.

And when Joe looked towards Dicky Hutt again, he had gone. The door was closing, the knob turning. The door clicked shut, and Joe could hear Dicky Hutt's feet tiptoeing away.

When Joe looked at his great grandmother again, she was sitting back in her chair. Her mouth was closed; the gibbering and the hooting and the wailing had ceased. She looked exhausted - or had she died?

But no, she was just looking unbelievably old.

He did not disturb her. He stood by her chair some time longer. Then he heard his parents calling over the house for him: they wanted to go home.

He moved his hand out of hers - the grasp was slack now: perhaps she had fallen asleep. He thought he wanted to kiss her goodbye; but then he did not want the feel of that century-old cheek against his lips.

So he simply slipped away from her and out of the room.

He never saw her again. Nearly a year later, at home, the news came of her death. Joe's mother said: "Poor old thing …"

Joe's father (whose grandmother great grandmother had been) said: "When I was a little boy, she was fun. I remember her. Jokey, then; full of tricks …"

Joe's mother said: "Well, she'd outlived all that. Outlived everything. Too old to be any use to herself - or to anyone else. A burden only."

Joe said nothing; but wished now that he had kissed her cheek, to say goodbye, and to thank her.

1 Joey is very afraid of his cousin Dicky but we are not told why. Can you suggest any reason? Could it be just an irrational fear?

2 Great grandmother does not see or hear much but it is likely from the story that she understands more than people think. What reason is there in the story for saying that?

3 When we get to the end of the story we are told that the grandmother was "fun, jokey, full of tricks". How does that information help us to understand what went on in the room?

4 At the very end of the story Joey wishes that he had kissed her cheek. What prevented him from doing so? Why does he wish now that he had?

5 Retell this story as if you were Joey now grown up telling his own children. Joey will of course have a better understanding of what went on.

Now try . . . . . .

6 Write your own story about a family gathering, in which a young person in the family has their own adventure while the rest of the party is taking place.

7 Who is the oldest person in your extended family? Write a brief portrait of that person, their character, and habits. Do you have relatives abroad? Draw your own family tree. You might try to extend this tree at home by talking to parents and other relatives.

REMINDER - In parenthesis.

When you write something as an aside in a sentence, you separate it off from the rest of the sentence by a pair of commas, or you may use dashes or brackets. There are some examples in the story.

When the day of the birthday came, everyone - just as Joe's mother had said - was there.

The children, if they were very young, clung to their parents.

Notice that there is a pair of punctuation marks in each case. You may leave out the pair of punctuation marks, and all the words within them, and still retain a sentence which makes logical, grammatical sense.

Can you find an example of the use of brackets in the story and any other examples of the use of parenthesis?

Ted Hughes invented a set of extraordinary relatives in his book, *Meet my Folks.* One of them was Jane, his sister, and the family were at pains to conceal her dark secret ...

My Sister Jane

And I say nothing - no, not a word
About our Jane. Haven't you heard
She's a bird, a bird, a bird, a bird.
Oh it never would do to let folks know
My sister's nothing but a great big crow.

Each day (we daren't send her to school)
She pulls on stockings of thick blue wool
To make her pin crow legs look right,
Then fits a wig of curls on tight,
And dark spectacles - a huge pair
To cover her very crowy stare.
Oh it never would do to let folks know
My sister's nothing but a great big crow.

When visitors come she sits upright
With her wings and her tail tucked out of sight.
They think her queer but extremely polite.
Then when the visitors have gone
She whips out her wings and with her wig on
Whirls through the house at the height of your head
Duck, duck, or she'll knock you dead.
Oh it never would do to let folks know
My sister's nothing but a great big crow.

Ted Hughes

(8) Have you noticed that different people seem to be more like one animal (in terms of appearance, habits, character) than another. Decide whether any of the people you know (relatives, friends in school) remind you of an animal. Try to say why.

(9) ☆ Try writing a poem about an extraordinary relative of your own. He or she may be actually an animal or bird or it may be someone who is like an animal or bird.

Go through these stages.

● FIRST Decide which relative to write about (father, sister, cousin, etc.).

● SECOND Choose which animal or bird they are - or are very much like (dragon, mouse, ostrich, etc.).

● THIRD Compose two rhyming lines with which to end each verse. Look at the endings of the verses in "My Sister Jane" for an example.

● FOURTH Write your own poem about how hard you try to stop people finding out about your relative and his/her strange habits.

Now try . . . . . .

10 Find and read other poems by Ted Hughes about members of his mythical family.

11 ☆ In groups of three or four, invent your own extraordinary family. Then each of you write up - in prose or verse - a description of one of the family. Illustrate these and make a wall display.

In this unit you will be considering the ways in which injustices can often happen, particularly when people are unwilling or unable to own up to what they have done. You will also learn about the importance of "context".

Here is a poem which consists of random excuses in response to what we can imagine are different accusations.

Not more excuses!

I lost it in the playground.
My pen ran out of ink.
My mum forgot to put it out.
I dropped it in the sink.

The roads were very busy.
I didn't get a mark.
My little sister tore it up.
I did it for a lark.

Sorry, I didn't hear you.
I left it in the car.
My mother said I couldn't play.
I cannot walk that far.

I cannot understand it.
My auntie came to stay.
Someone must have pinched my book.
I wasn't taught that way.

Patricia Hollingsworth

1. Read this poem aloud and write a sentence which corresponds with each of the lines. These should describe what the teacher might have said to prompt these replies. Shape your lines into a poem called "Teaching".

2. Now that you have the idea of writing what people are saying without defining the context (i.e. where it is happening, who is speaking, etc), put the title "Arriving Late" and write different excuses in the same way. Try situations other than ones about school.

3. Here are four lines of a simple conversation between two people without the context.

   A: "I'm sorry, I really am, but it wasn't my fault."
   B: "We're lucky the thing didn't come down."
   A: "I'll have it fixed in a moment."
   B: "Don't worry. I'll do it."

   ● Give this speech a context. Who is speaking? Where are they? What are they talking about?
   ● Read the exchange in four different ways, giving a different emphasis each time by changing the tone. Suggested versions:
   ● Both A and B are angry. Neither A nor B is angry. A is rather cross but B is calm. A is very apologetic but B is cross.
   ● Can you think of any others?

In this poem the writer is denying something in each verse but, at the same time, betraying guilt. We could say there is self deception going on.

Don't Blame Me

You stole my pen a year ago,
So isn't it quite fair
For me to borrow yours - you see,
I thought you wouldn't care.

It wasn't me who broke your vase,
I know you said "Don't touch".
I couldn't reach it - anyway,
It wasn't worth that much.

I know I took some money,
But I wouldn't call it theft.
I had a mind to put it back,
And you had plenty left.

I know I gave you poison,
But I didn't think you'd mind.
I did think it would kill you,
But I did it to be kind.

Chris Evans

(4) Go through each verse in the poem identifying the key words which indicate:
a) what the speaker is trying to believe, and
b) what is actually the case.

(5) Take any of these verses and create a full context for it. Decide what has happened, who is speaking, what are the full circumstances.

(6) In pairs choose one of the verses and act out what happened when the individual was accused. Do not turn the exchange into a major row but concentrate on one person trying to make an excuse and the other firmly refusing to accept it.

(7) Write about an occasion when you did something wrong and felt unable to admit to it.

8.2 Rough Justice.

You will need to be in groups of five or six for reading this short one act play. Give the parts out and read it once through fairly quickly.

Characters: Mrs Feather - teacher. Sandra, Carol, Matthew, Ben, pupils. Mr Thompson - teacher.

Mrs F: For the last time I want one of you to own up - who broke it?

Matthew: It wasn't us, Miss - anyone could have done it.

Mrs F: You were in the room when I got here. You know the rule - you have to wait outside. What were you doing in here anyway?

Sandra: Miss, we only came in to get the books out.

Matthew: Yeah, ''Noddy goes to town''.

Carol: *(Giggles)* We didn't break your bust Miss, we didn't go near it.

Mrs F: It's nothing to laugh at. That sculpture was not cheap and it wasn't mine. It was a present to the school. The Head's going to be furious. Didn't you see the sign, ''Do Not Touch''?

Matthew: None of us can read, Miss.

Mrs F: Now for the last time, who broke it? Was it you Ben?

Ben: No it wasn't. Why do I always get the blame?

Mrs F: I'm not saying it was you - but someone did it. Who came into the room first?

Matthew: I have to own up Miss. *(Raises arm)* It was Carol. *(Suddenly points to Carol)*

Carol: No it wasn't, liar. You and Ben came in before us.

Matthew: Stop snitching, scabby.

Carol: Tea-bag, freckle face.

Mrs F: Stop it. You don't seem to realise the seriousness of this. You have caused deliberate damage to a piece of valuable school property.

Ben: Deliberate, what do you mean deliberate?

Mrs F: So you agree that you broke it? If it was an accident the best thing you can do is own up.

Ben: I didn't say we did it - but if we did, it wouldn't have been deliberate.

Carol: That's a big word for you, cloth-head.

Ben: Rat-bag.

Sandra: Miss, we did come in the room and we were larking about but we didn't break the statue.

Mrs F: Now we're getting somewhere. Tell me this at least, did you go near the bust at all?

Sandra: Ben put a hat on it, Miss.

Matthew: *(Under his breath)* Don't you mean a bra?

Mrs F: Well Ben, did you?

Ben: I was only larking about, I put one of those plastic bowls on it like a helmet. But I didn't break it.

Mrs F: Surely you'd have noticed that its ear was missing if you didn't do it.

Matthew: *(Laughing)* You could pretend it's Van Gogh.

Carol: 'Ere, ere, what's all this then?

Matthew: I can't 'ear you, I haven't got an ear.

Mrs F: *(Shouts and pupils suddenly become serious)* Now that's enough. You think this is some kind of joke. I'm warning you that if you don't own up I'm going for the Head - I'll even consider calling the police. I'm going outside this room - you can discuss it yourselves - but when I come back I want an answer. The bell will go soon and I'm not letting you go home until someone owns up. *(Leaves the room)*

Carol: Old boot. I hate her and I hate this lesson. Why can't we stay with the rest of the class?

Matthew: Cos we're thick.

Sandra: I think whoever did it should own up.

Matthew: Go on then.

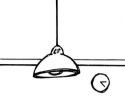

Carol: I wasn't near it. But I want to go home. I'm going out tonight.

Sandra: With that lad who smells? What's his name, Peter Peckitt?

Matthew: You'll have to watch YOUR bust.

Carol: Don't be rude.

Sandra: Look, be serious. Did you do it, Ben? It was you who was messing about with the thing and none of us was near you.

Matthew: Yeah, why don't you just own up? Then we can all go home.

Sandra: She won't do much, she never does.

Ben: But I didn't do it.

Carol: You must have.

Sandra: You were the only one near it.

Carol: Own up.

Matthew: Chicken. *(Flaps arms and makes a noise like a chicken as teacher walks in - pretends he was coughing)*

Mrs F: This is your last chance. I have a letter here I'm going to get typed and send to your parents - it explains the circumstances and invites them to come to the school to discuss the matter.

Matthew: You'll never find Ben's mum to give it to her - she's disappeared.

Carol: You could try down the sewers. *(Ben tries to kick her)*

Matthew: He's so thick maybe he forgot he did it.

Mrs F: Now the bell's gone. I'm keeping you here until someone owns up. It had to be one of you. Nobody else came into the room. If you own up now that will be an end of the matter, nothing more will be said. I'd rather have it cleared up.

Sandra: Ben wants to say something, Miss.

Mrs F: At last, Ben if you own up now you'll save yourself a great deal of trouble in the long run. Did you break it?

Ben: Yes, Miss.

Mrs F: Right, you stay behind, the rest of you can go. *(During this speech Ben tries to interrupt a few times but cannot get a word in. He is obviously very angry but Mrs Feather does not really notice.)* Ben, you ought to be ashamed of yourself. It is not so much breaking the sculpture but lying to me for so long is what is really disappointing. You 've proved yourself to be a sneaky, low, cowardly individual. One thing people respect, Ben, is courage. You'll never make friends if you carry on like this. You wasted everybody's time in the class and we got no work done in this lesson. How are you going to make progress with this kind of behaviour? Now I am going to say no more about the breakage, although I'll think twice before I can believe anything you say in future. I am going to write to your father because I think we need to talk about your general attitude. Now I want you to go home from here and think about what I've said. I hope you've learned something from today - have you?

Ben: Yes, Miss.

Mrs F: Off you go. *(Ben leaves and another teacher comes in the door)*

Mr T: Oh, Jan, I'm glad I caught you before you left. That bust of Lincoln - I'm so sorry I came in here before the start of last lesson and as I was moving it to get in the cupboard it dropped on the desk. I've just been over to the technical department to get some glue to fix it. It's a clean break so it should repair easily. Are you listening?

Mrs F: *(Very slowly and deliberately)* You're wrong. You didn't break it - a boy in my class broke it when he was messing about before the start of the lesson. It was definitely him. I'm not going to punish him though - it was an accident.

Mr T: *(Glad to have responsibility shifted a little away from him)* I'm sure I did it. But what does it really matter as long as we can get it fixed? This stuff dries in minutes and when it's standing in the school hall you'll never be able to tell.

Mrs F: *(Softly)* He's a really clumsy boy, really clumsy.

John Essler

Rough Justice.

1 Having read through the play once your next task is to read it with more expression or, better still, act it out. In order to do so you will find the following activities useful.

✓ A play will often have notes on each of the characters at the start, describing what they are like as people so the actors will know how to act the part. Write notes of two or three lines for each of the five central characters in the play, basing them on what you have read. You might consider whether it would be a good idea to have any of the characters be of different nationalities.

✓ Decide whether your original casting (i.e. giving parts to different people in the group) was the right one. If not, change the parts. What makes one part seem to suit one person more than another?

✓ Go through the play writing notes on what each of the characters should be doing at different points in the play, e.g. Mrs Feather might be tidying up as she is talking. Are the pupils seated or standing? Do the characters point to the sculpture or pick it up at any stage?

☆ ✓ Go through the play writing notes on how particular lines should be said. The writer has given some clues but you should annotate (i.e. makes notes on) every line you have to say.

✓ Work out a simple classroom scene on paper in a diagrammatic form. Show where the characters will be placed and what props will be needed.

✓ This play was written for three males and three females but it could easily be adapted for your group. Decide if that is necessary and if it is adapt it accordingly.

2 There are a number of ways in which the incident could be continued in improvised role play or in a scripted form. Try out some of the following situations to see what might have happened:
- Father's reaction with Ben when he gets the letter and his visit to the school.
- Meeting between Mrs Feather and Mr Thompson the next day when the latter insists that he broke the sculpture.
- Next day at school when Ben, Sandra, Carol and Matthew meet.
- Head notices the crack and asks to see Mrs Feather - that starts a reopening of the case.

3 What made Ben admit to something which he had not done? List the different pressures on him which made him confess.

4 Why was Mrs Feather so keen to have someone confess? At the start of the scene she says, "The Head's going to be furious." Does this give us a clue?

5 Here is the letter which Mrs Feather wrote to Ben's father that night. She did not post it because she decided that she should tone it down and improve the style - too much repetition and some awkward sentences. Write her second draft.

Dear Mr. Hedley,

I am writing to you over the behaviour of your son Ben who is in my remedial class and tutor group. His behaviour is absolutely atrocious, worse than anyone else's behaviour in the class. If he continues to behave in the way he is at the moment he will never make sufficient progress. He does not concentrate enough in class and his reading is not improving. I am also a bit concerned about his manner in class. He is not really a very truthful boy and, although I have no particular incident in mind, he gives the impression of being constantly untruthful.

Please come to the school to discuss this matter as soon as you can.

Yours sincerely

Mrs J. Feather.

6 At one point Mrs Feather says "I hope you've learned something from today". This could be described as a case of "dramatic irony". This term is used to refer to a moment in a play when a character says some lines which actually mean far more to the audience than the character who is speaking the lines. What could Ben be said to have actually learned from the day?

7 In the scene the pupils make different references either directly or indirectly to their own intelligence. Find them and list them. Are there any indications in the scene that, despite what they say themselves, it is clear that the pupils are far from being "thick"?

8 Explain the significance of the very last line of the play.

Now try . . . . . .

9 ☆ Write a play of your own based on a simple scene which takes place in one room with a small number of characters.

8.3 Second Opinion.

There is a famous murder case which took place in 1951 in London. Timothy Evans, a young Welsh man, admitted to the murder of his wife and young baby even though he had not committed the crime. He was hanged. Some years later John Christie was convicted of the murder. He was also hanged and Evans was granted a pardon.

What made Evans confess? Nobody knows exactly but these are some of the circumstances. Evans thought his wife had died in an operation which he had allowed Christie to perform in the house (Christie had been a medical orderly) - he therefore felt guilty. The police were convinced Evans was guilty and apparently put enormous pressure on him to confess. Evans was confused, fatigued and reportedly of limited intelligence.

1 Invent your own case in which someone confesses to something they have not done. It is up to you whether it takes place in school or not.

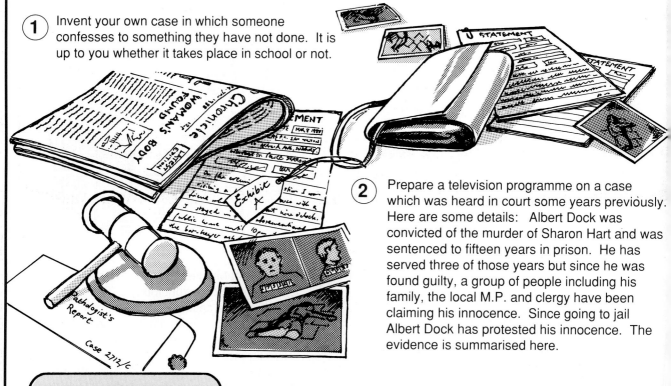

2 Prepare a television programme on a case which was heard in court some years previously. Here are some details: Albert Dock was convicted of the murder of Sharon Hart and was sentenced to fifteen years in prison. He has served three of those years but since he was found guilty, a group of people including his family, the local M.P. and clergy have been claiming his innocence. Since going to jail Albert Dock has protested his innocence. The evidence is summarised here.

The Original Case

The body of Sharon Hart was found in a cul de sac. She had been strangled and her handbag stolen. Albert Dock did not know the victim but he was convicted on the following circumstantial evidence.

1. He had been drinking in the George and Dragon pub and had been seen leaving in a drunken state at 10.00 p.m. after the barman had refused to give him credit; Albert had run out of money.
2. A Mrs Butler swore that she saw Albert Dock struggling with the victim while she was waiting for a bus. A bus came along and she jumped on thinking it was a simple argument between boyfriend and girlfriend. It was later when she read about the murder that she told the police.
3. The handbag was found dumped in a garden which Albert would have passed by on the way to his house.
4. Albert admitted that he might have committed the crime in one police interview but he later retracted that statement.

The New Case

1. Witnesses say that Albert was really staggering when he left the pub. A fit young girl (as Sharon Hart was) could very likely have pushed him off and run away.
2. The line of vision from the bus stop would not have allowed Mrs Butler to actually see the struggle. She has been questioned by newspaper reporters and now admits that she heard rather than saw the struggle and picked Albert Dock out of a line-up because she had seen him drunk on the road that night. She admits her imagination got the better of her slightly.
3. If Albert in his drunken state had murdered for money for drink (which was the prosecution case), why did he not return to the pub to spend it? Those actions would have been strange but no stranger than the prosecution claim that Albert had murdered for money for drink.
4. Albert was drunk and, under police pressure, had said that he might have committed the crime. However, if he was so drunk not to remember his actions he would hardly have been able to do so.
5. A new witness who lives in the cul de sac now claims that she saw someone running and leaping over the fence which leads to the railway line. By coincidence she emigrated the day after the murder, not realising what had happened, and was missed in the house to house search.

(3) Your job is to present the television programme which gives the facts of the original case and also the new evidence.
- You could interview the new witnesses and include any extra details you feel would make the case more interesting.
- You could prepare a written script or give an outline of what you are going to improvise.
- You might find it helpful to structure the programme in terms of different location, for different scenes, e.g. outside a prison, in the studio with map, where the body was found, in the studio for a discussion.

LOCATION: Outside prison.

SHOT: Reporter talking to camera. Walk forward during talk so that prison looms up in the background.

SCRIPT: Inside these prison walls Mr Dock is now beginning the third year of a prison sentence which he received for the murder of a young girl, Sharon Hart. All through the trial and ever since he has protested his innocence. Tonight we reveal startling new evidence which indicates that Albert Dock could not possibly have committed the murder. Let us go back to the night of August 5th three years ago ...

9.1 Community Life.

In this unit you will be looking at communities of people. You will need to think hard about characters, places and stories.

1 Where would you choose to live? Make a list of the reasons for your choice. Compare your decisions with those of the rest of the class.

2 In which of these locations would you choose to set a Soap Opera? Is it the same as your answer to the first question?

3 Can you think of any Soap Operas on television or on radio which are set in locations like these?

4 What are the advantages and disadvantages of each location for the setting of a Soap Opera?

Now try . . . . . .

5 Can you suggest other locations, not shown here, which would be suitable for the setting of a Soap Opera?

Almost everyone seems to watch Soap Operas on television or listen to them on the radio at some time or other. All Soap Operas have three things in common.

✓ **Characters.** Clearly drawn characters, easily recognisable. You can often guess what they will do or say in certain situations because you feel you know them. There is often a villain that everyone hates.

✓ **Locations.** There are quite a small number of places in which you see the characters each week. These are usually places where the people in the story would meet together naturally.

✓ **Plot.** There is a lot of action. Every episode has plenty happening in it.

⑥ Carry out a survey to find out which are the favourite Soap Operas in your class.
Ask one person to speak on behalf of each one chosen to say what they like about it. Do you all like the same characters?

⑦ Take your favourite Soap Opera.
● Write down the character you like most and what you like about her/him.
● Write down the character you dislike most and what you dislike about her/him.
● Compare your notes with a friend.
● How much do you know about where your chosen Soap Opera takes place? The action probably takes place mainly in a few locations. Can you list them?
● How many are there? How well can you describe the area where your chosen Soap Opera takes place?

Now try . . . . . .

8 Work in small groups of 3 or 4 to create your own community. You will have to decide between you:
● The place where your community lives.
● The people who live there and their relationships with each other.
● Stories about their lives.
Your first decision is whether your community lives in a village or a town. If you decide on a village, turn to page 70. If you decide on a town or city, turn to page 72.

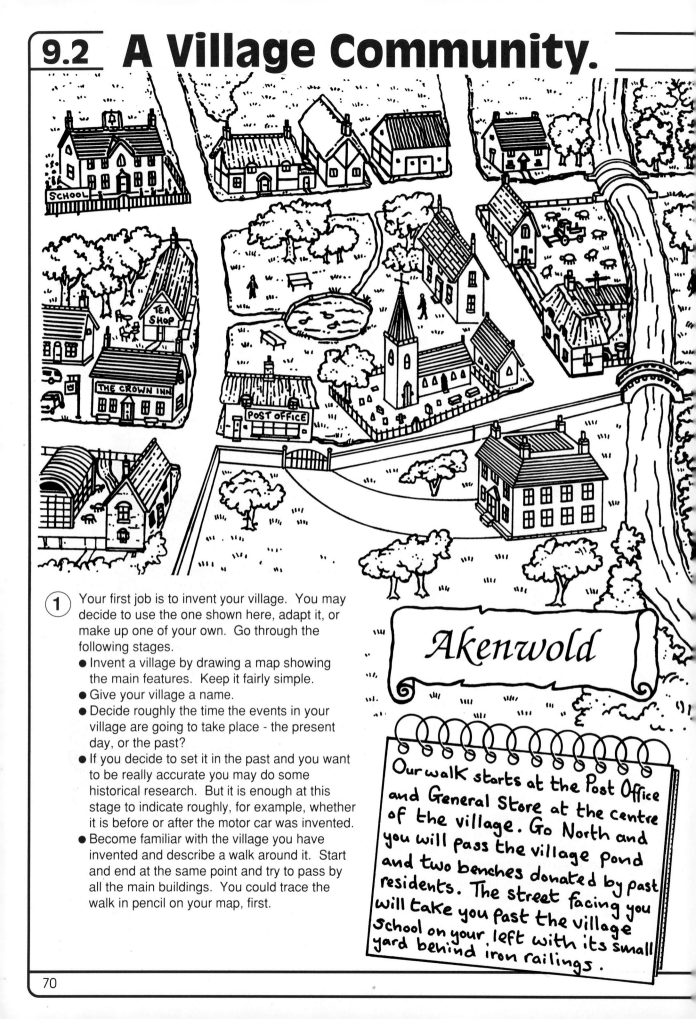

Akenwold

① Your first job is to invent your village. You may decide to use the one shown here, adapt it, or make up one of your own. Go through the following stages.

- Invent a village by drawing a map showing the main features. Keep it fairly simple.
- Give your village a name.
- Decide roughly the time the events in your village are going to take place - the present day, or the past?
- If you decide to set it in the past and you want to be really accurate you may do some historical research. But it is enough at this stage to indicate roughly, for example, whether it is before or after the motor car was invented.
- Become familiar with the village you have invented and describe a walk around it. Start and end at the same point and try to pass by all the main buildings. You could trace the walk in pencil on your map, first.

Our walk starts at the Post Office and General Store at the centre of the village. Go North and you will pass the village pond and two benches donated by past residents. The street facing you will take you past the village school on your left with its small yard behind iron railings.

② THE POPULATION

Your next task is to create the characters who live in the village and to decide who you are each going to be. You will need to decide on the characters as a group, and allocate the task of writing up a few notes on each.

Here are a few characters you might choose, but think of others to add to your list. Nothing has been written about their personalities, so you will need to do this.

Farmers, vicar, shopkeeper, shepherd, veterinary surgeon, gardener, farmworkers (men and women), odd-jobber, blacksmith, schoolteacher, thatcher, saddler, housewives, gravedigger.

● Describe who you are in the village and invent as much detail as you can about your character: where you live, how long you have been in the village, whether you have a family. Do this in note form and then write about yourself in the first person.
For example:- *My name is Sidney Miller and I work as the village blacksmith ...*
● Decide where you live and work and where these places are on your map. Find out who lives near you and works with you. Are you friendly, good-tempered, or do you like to keep yourself to yourself?

③ RELATIONSHIPS

Your next task is to work out something about the relationships you have with people in your village. You will need to discuss these as a group so that you are consistent. It is no good saying that you are a close friend of the publican if he claims that you are his enemy! You will have to find a way of negotiating the relationships.

Mrs Baker owns the local store and post office and she is a good friend of mine. We went to school together years ago and now we often meet in the evenings to talk over old times. The trouble is that she has that snotty Doreen Walker from Highcombe Grange working for her. I had a row with her a year ago when she gave me the wrong change and I've never really spoken to her properly since. It's a bit awkward when I go in the shop if Linda (Mrs Baker) isn't there.

④ Now your village is ready for action. To familiarise yourself with it, write a fairly full diary of a typical day of your life in the village. Make sure you meet plenty of other village people. Then turn to page 74.

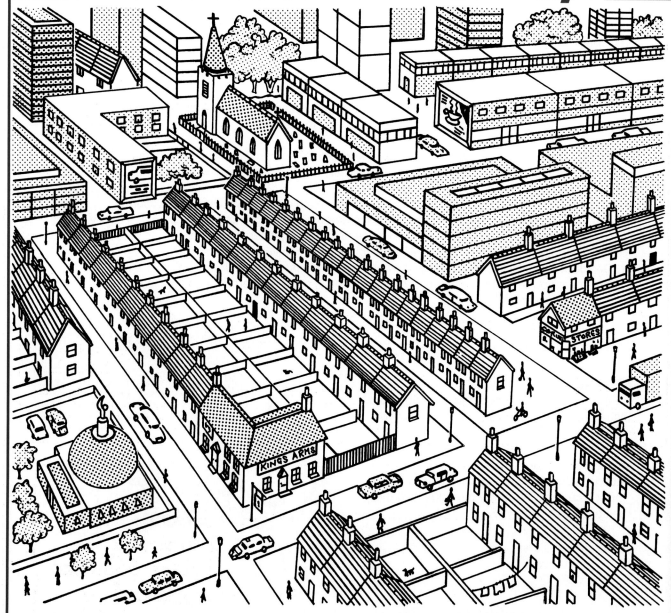

(1) You cannot invent a whole town or city, so first decide on the area in which your characters live. You may decide to use the one shown here, adapt it, or make up your own.
Go through the following stages.

● Invent your area by drawing a map showing the main features. Keep it to quite a small area - just a few streets will be enough.

● Name your city/town, and also all the streets in your area.

● In order to become familiar with the area you have invented, describe a walk round it. Start and end at the same point, and try to pass all the main buildings.

Our walk starts outside the King's Arms in Ruby street. Turn right, past the mosque along Diamond Street. You will see a row of small terraced houses on each side of you......

② THE POPULATION

Now create the characters who live in the area and decide who you are going to be. Limit your choice to not more than 10 main people. You can always add minor characters later if you wish.

Here is a sample of the characters you might choose. You can think of others to add to the list.

PAUL SIDHU (38). EX-PROFESSIONAL FOOTBALLER, NOW MANAGING A LOCAL SPORTS COMPLEX. MARRIED WITH ONE DAUGHTER. DREAMS OF MAKING A COMEBACK.

SHARON LEPAGE (22). TELEVISION CAMERA OPERATOR AT NEARBY STUDIOS. UNMARRIED. SINGS IN A FRIEND'S BAND AND IS HOPING TO CUT A RECORD LATER IN THE YEAR.

MARGARET MORRIS (65). LECTURER IN POLITICS. WIDOW WITH ONE GRANDCHILD. FORMER MAYOR. HAS BEEN ARRESTED TWICE THIS YEAR FOR DISTURBANCES CAUSED AT LOCAL DEMONSTRATIONS.

③ Describe who you are in this community and invent as much detail as you can about your character: where you live, how long you have lived there, whether you have a family, whether you are friendly or lonely. Do this in note form and then write about yourself in the first person. For example: *My name is Linda Thompson and I am a student at the Further Education College.*

④ RELATIONSHIPS

Work out something about the relationships you have with the other characters in your community.
For example: *Next door to me live three Polytechnic students. I'm quite friendly with Winston, but Tracey and Mattie have more or less ignored me ever since I complained about a noisy party late one night ...*

⑤ A DAY IN MY LIFE.

What is it like to live in your community? Write a very full diary entry for one day. In it you will meet all the main characters in your community, so your reader will really know what it is like to live there.

MONDAY :

Woken up at 6.30 this morning as Winston slammed his front door. Crawled out of bed, had breakfast and then went out to shop for paper. Tom Eversley told me about the trouble in Diamond Street last night...

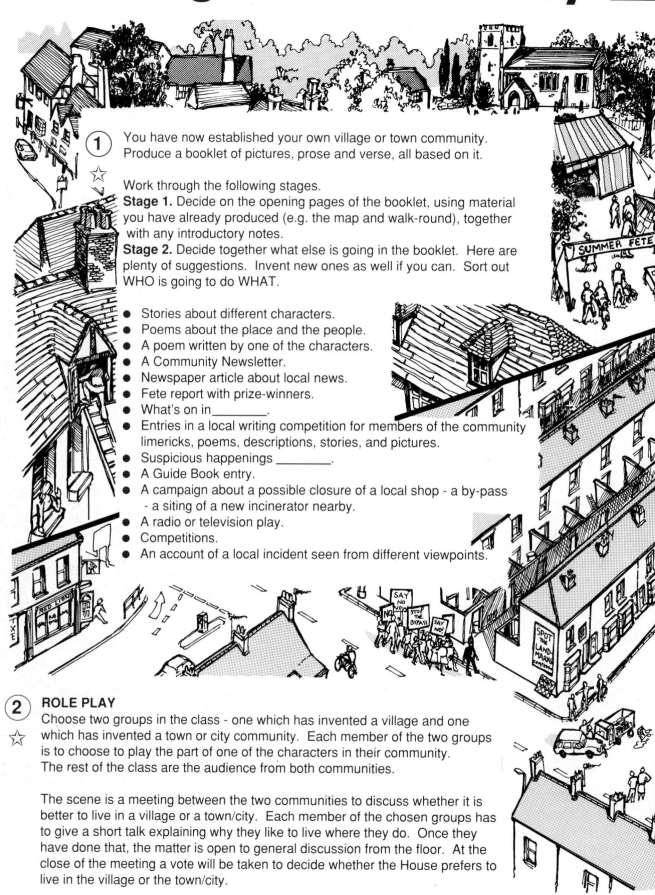

9.4 Living in a Community.

1 You have now established your own village or town community. Produce a booklet of pictures, prose and verse, all based on it.

Work through the following stages.

Stage 1. Decide on the opening pages of the booklet, using material you have already produced (e.g. the map and walk-round), together with any introductory notes.

Stage 2. Decide together what else is going in the booklet. Here are plenty of suggestions. Invent new ones as well if you can. Sort out WHO is going to do WHAT.

- Stories about different characters.
- Poems about the place and the people.
- A poem written by one of the characters.
- A Community Newsletter.
- Newspaper article about local news.
- Fete report with prize-winners.
- What's on in _____.
- Entries in a local writing competition for members of the community limericks, poems, descriptions, stories, and pictures.
- Suspicious happenings _____.
- A Guide Book entry.
- A campaign about a possible closure of a local shop - a by-pass - a siting of a new incinerator nearby.
- A radio or television play.
- Competitions.
- An account of a local incident seen from different viewpoints.

2 **ROLE PLAY**

Choose two groups in the class - one which has invented a village and one which has invented a town or city community. Each member of the two groups is to choose to play the part of one of the characters in their community. The rest of the class are the audience from both communities.

The scene is a meeting between the two communities to discuss whether it is better to live in a village or a town/city. Each member of the chosen groups has to give a short talk explaining why they like to live where they do. Once they have done that, the matter is open to general discussion from the floor. At the close of the meeting a vote will be taken to decide whether the House prefers to live in the village or the town/city.

Below is the opening of the novel *Claudine* by Colette. Colette actually grew up in Saint-Sauveur-en-Puisaye, but she puts a lot of her own feeling for her home village into the description by Claudine.

My name is Claudine. I live in Montigny; I was born there in 1884; I shall probably not die there. My "Manual of Departmental Geography" expresses itself thus: 'Montigny-en-Frenois, a pretty little town of 1,950 inhabitants, built in tiers above the Thaize; its well-preserved Saracen tower is worthy of note ...' To me, those descriptions are totally meaningless! To begin with, the Thaize doesn't exist. Of course I know it's supposed to run through the meadows under the level-crossing but you won't find enough water there in any season to give a sparrow a foot-bath. Montigny 'built in tiers'? No, that's not how I see it; to my mind, the houses just tumble haphazard from the top of the hill to the bottom of the valley. They rise one above the other, like a staircase, leading up to a big chateau that was rebuilt under Louis XV and is already more dilapidated than the squat, ivy-sheathed Saracen tower that crumbles away from the top a trifle more every day. Montigny is a village, not a town: its streets, thank heaven, are not paved; the showers roll down them in little torrents that dry up in a couple of hours; it is a village, not even a very pretty village, but, all the same, I adore it.

The charm, the delight of this countryside composed of hills and of valleys so narrow that some are ravines, lies in the woods - the deep, encroaching woods that ripple and wave away into the distance as far as you can see ... Green meadows make rifts in them here and there, so do little patches of cultivation. But these do not amount to much, for the magnificent woods devour everything. As a result, this lovely region is atrociously poor and its few scattered farms provide just the requisite number of red roofs to set off the velvety green of the woods.

Dear woods! I know them all; I've scoured them so often. There are the copses, where bushes spitefully catch your face as you pass. Those are full of sun and strawberries and lilies-of-the-valley; they are also full of snakes. I've shuddered there with choking terror at the sight of those dreadful, smooth, cold little bodies gliding just in front of my feet. Dozens of times near the 'rose-mallow' I've stopped still, panting, when I've found a well-behaved grass snake under my hand. It would be neatly coiled up like a snail-shell, with its head raised and its little golden eyes staring at me: it was not dangerous, but how it frightened me! But never mind all that: I shall always end up by going back there, alone or with my friends.

3 Reread this extract from *"Claudine"* and then write down as quickly as you can about six or eight words which summarise the way Claudine feels about the area in which she lives.

4 Think back to the character you chose to be in the community you invented. Write down about six or eight words which summarise the way he or she feels about the area in which he or she lives.

Now try . . . . . .

5 Write two or three paragraphs as if you were this character. Try to give a vivid overall impression of your area like Claudine does.

This unit is about discoveries. You will be finding out about some famous discoveries and investigating your own talents.

If someone found treasure in your garden, whose property would it be?
In 1943, a ploughman called Gordon Butcher found some buried silver treasure near Mildenhall in Suffolk. It was Roman silver, nearly 2000 years old, and turned out to be one of the greatest treasures ever found in the British Isles. It is now in the British Museum in London. Roald Dahl's short story, *The Mildenhall Treasure*, reports exactly what happened, how the treasure was discovered, and why the discovery was kept secret for three years.

A

And suddenly, as the gloved fingers scraped away a final handful of black earth, he caught sight of something flat, like the rim of a huge thick plate, sticking up out of the soil. He rubbed the rim with his fingers, and he rubbed again. Then all at once, the rim gave off a greenish glint, and Gordon Butcher bent his head closer and closer still, peering down into the little hole he had dug with his hands.

For one last time, he rubbed the rim clean with his fingers, and in a flash of light, he saw clearly the unmistakable blue-green crust of ancient buried metal, and his heart stood still.

It should be explained here that farmers in this part of Suffolk, and particularly in the Mildenhall area, have for years been turning up ancient objects from the soil. Flint arrowheads from very long ago have been found in considerable numbers, but more interesting than that, Roman pottery and Roman implements have also been found. It is known that Romans favoured this part of the country during their occupation of Britain, and all local farmers are therefore well aware of the possibility of finding something interesting during a day's work. And so there was a kind of permanent awareness among Mildenhall people of the presence of treasure underneath the earth of their land.

Gordon Butcher was ploughing the field for a man called Ford, but the owner of the land was called Rolfe. Unlike Butcher, Ford knew the find might be valuable.

B

Ford knelt down beside the front of the plough and peered into the small hole Gordon Butcher had dug with his hands. He touched the rim of green-blue metal with a gloved finger. He scraped away a bit more earth. He leaned farther forward so that his pointed nose was right down the hole. He ran his fingers over the rough green surface. Then he stood up and said, "Let's get the plough out of the way and do some digging." Although there were fireworks exploding in his head and shivers running all over his body, Ford kept his voice very soft and casual. Between them they pulled the plough back a couple of yards.

"Give me the spade," Ford said, and he began cautiously to dig the soil away in a circle about three feet in diameter around the exposed patch of metal.

When the hole was two feet deep, he threw away the spade and used his hands. He knelt down and scraped the soil away, and gradually the little patch of metal grew and grew until at last there lay exposed before them the great round disc of an enormous plate. It was fully twenty-four inches in diameter. The lower point of the plough had just caught the raised centre rim of the plate, for one could see the dent.

Carefully Ford lifted it out of the hole. He got to his feet and stood wiping the soil away from it, turning it over and over in his hands. There was nothing much to see, for the whole surface was crusted over with a thick layer of a hard greenish-blue substance. But he knew that it was an enormous plate or dish of great weight and thickness. It weighed about eighteen pounds!

Ford stood in the field of yellow barley stubble and gazed at the huge plate. His hands began to shake. A tremendous and almost unbearable excitement started boiling up inside him, and it was not easy for him to hide it. But he did his best.

"Some sort of dish," he said.

Butcher was kneeling on the ground beside the hole. "Must be pretty old," he said.

"Could be old," Ford said. "But it's all rusted up and eaten away."

"That don't look like rust to me," Butcher said. "That greenish stuff isn't rust. It's something else."

"It's green rust," Ford said rather superbly, and that ended the discussion.

Butcher, still on his knees, was poking about casually in the now three-foot-wide hole with his gloved hands. "There's another one down there," he said.

Instantly, Ford laid the great dish on the ground.

He knelt beside Butcher, and within minutes they had unearthed a second large green-encrusted plate. This one was a shade smaller than the first, and deeper. More of a bowl than a dish.

Ford stood up and held the new find in his hands. Another heavy one. And now he knew for certain they were on to something absolutely tremendous. They were on to Roman treasure, and almost without question it was pure silver. Two things pointed to it being pure silver. First the weight, and second, the particular type of green crust caused by oxidisation. How often is a piece of Roman silver discovered in the world?

Almost never any more.

And have pieces as large as this EVER been unearthed before?

Ford wasn't sure, but he very much doubted it.

Worth millions, it must be.

Worth literally millions of pounds.

Silver treasure from Mildenhall.

1. Extract **A**. To make a discovery you need to NOTICE DETAILS and UNDERSTAND THE SIGNIFICANCE. What made Butcher think he was on to something?
Extract **B**. Now Ford is in charge. Imagine you are Ford and write down a list of ALL the evidence which makes you think this is going to be a major discovery. Why does Ford want to hide his excitement from Butcher?

2. Imagine that Butcher goes home and tells his wife what has happened and that Ford has taken the treasure with him. She is shrewder than him. Write out the conversation they had.

3. Role-play a scene in which Butcher meets Ford now that he knows it is really treasure.

4. Now you know the stark facts of the story, give your judgement and reasons as to what should happen to: the treasure, Gordon Butcher, Ford, Rolfe.

5. If you look at page 96, you will find a summary of the relevant law. Now, what do you think should happen to each of the three men? To find out what actually happened you will need to read Roald Dahl's story.

FACT: At Sutton Hoo, treasure was buried many hundreds of years ago at the centre of a burial mound.
FACT: In the middle ages, treasure-hunters dug into the middle of the mound but found no treasure.
FACT: In 1939, archaelogists dug into the mound and found a large amount of treasure.
Can you think of an explanation?

At Sutton Hoo, the mound was raised over a complete ship. Originally it would have covered the entire ship evenly, but the mound had later been eroded or dug away at one end. When treasure-hunters dug into the mound in the middle ages they assumed they were in the middle and missed the treasure. It was not until 1939 that it was uncovered. Who had been buried in the mound?

When they began to dig, they came across rusty iron rivets and stains in the sand; the stains had once been the planks of a boat, which they worked out had been 27 metres long. They also found rich treasure, including weapons, armour, silver bowls, remains of clothes and their rich trimmings like a solid-gold belt buckle weighing more than 400 grammes, jewellery and coins. But no trace of a body was found.

Can you think who might have been buried there? Or, if there was a body in the mound, what had happened to it?

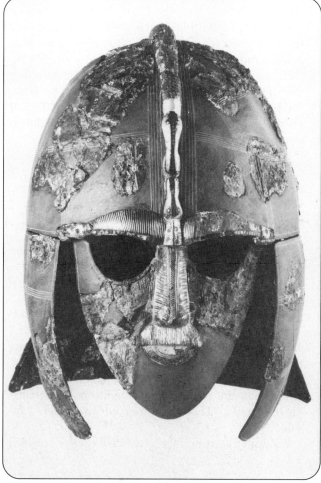

Treasure from the Sutton Hoo ship burial.

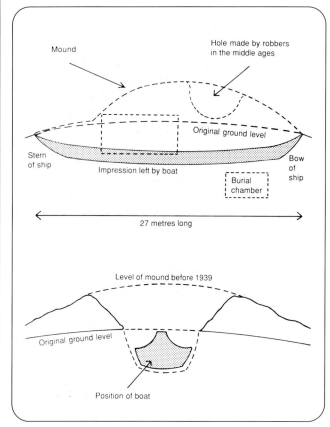

Sections through the Sutton Hoo ship burial.

On 14th August 1939, a Coroner's inquest was held to decide whether the Sutton Hoo treasure was Treasure Trove or not. The jury heard that the burial must have been common knowledge at the time because of the work force needed to drag such a large ship half a mile overland.

Furthermore, extracts from an almost contemporary poem describing funeral rights convinced them that the objects had not been lost and there was never any intention to recover them. For these two reasons the finds were declared NOT to be Treasure Trove, whereupon they became the property of the landowner, Mrs Pretty. She then presented the whole find to the nation, so the end result was the same.

The extracts below are from a poem called *Beowulf,* written 70 or so years after the seventh century Sutton Hoo burial. No part of it describes ship burials, but two extracts may give us clues about the mysteries of Sutton Hoo. Passage **A** describes how a dead chief was consigned to the sea. Passage **B** describes the raising of a mound, or barrow, over the remains of Beowulf himself. Both passages have been translated into modern English.

A

There in the harbour stood the ring-prowed ship,
the prince's vessel, shrouded in ice and eager to sail;
and then they laid their dear lord,
the giver of rings, deep within the ship
by the mast in majesty; many treasures
and adornments from far and wide were
gathered there.
I never heard of a ship equipped more handsomely
with weapons and war-gear,
swords and corslets; on his breast
lay countless treasures that were to travel far
with him into the waves' domain.
They gave him great ornaments, gifts
no less magnificent than those men had given him
long before, when they sent him alone,
child as he was, across the stretch of the seas.
Then high above his head they placed
a golden banner and let the waves bear him,
bequeathed him to the sea; their hearts were grieving,
their minds mourning. Mighty men
beneath the heavens, rulers in the hall.

B

Then the Geats built a barrow on the headland
it was high and broad, visible from far
to all seafarers; in ten days they built the beacon
for that courageous man; and they constructed
as noble an enclosure as wise men
could devise, to enshrine the ashes.
They buried rings and brooches in the barrow,
all those adornments that brave men
had brought out from the hoard after Beowulf died.
They bequeathed the gleaming gold, treasure of men,
to the earth, and there it still remains,
as useless to men as it was before.

(1) Discuss the two passages so that you are sure of what is happening in both. What do you think the poet means by the last sentence in each one? Which parts would have convinced the jury members that the Sutton Hoo treasure was not Treasure Trove, do you think?

(2) Do you think it is right that we should dig up such treasures when the people who buried them clearly intended that they should remain there for ever?

Now try . . . . . .

3 Look back at the two extracts from "*Beowulf*". Imagine that you are among the crowd at EITHER the ship ceremony OR the burial of Beowulf. Continue the free verse by describing your sad and lonely journey home.

1 ☆ In pairs prepare a booklet to explain to museum visitors the meaning of the Sutton Hoo treasure. The booklet is intended to answer all the questions visitors are likely to ask. So, instead of being in sections, it is to consist of a series of questions and answers.

You will need to decide:
1. What questions to ask.
2. The order of the questions.

Write out the questions and your answers. Most of your answers will, of course, be several sentences long.

Here are some questions you might use, but think up many more for yourselves.

- Why was the treasure still there when so many barrows had been robbed by earlier treasure hunters?
- Why was no body ever found in what was apparently a funeral burial?
- Why were treasures buried when someone died?
- Why were weapons buried?

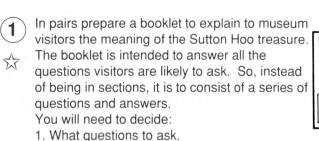

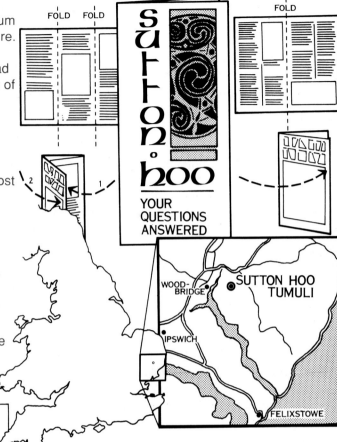

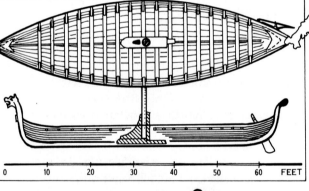

Now try . . . . . .

2 Design a poster for an exhibition of buried treasure.

3 Much has been written about Sutton Hoo. You may find out more about it if you look in your school and local libraries. The British Museum has published well-illustrated material about it.

4 ☆ You could do some research about local buried treasure. Apart from the Mildenhall and Sutton Hoo finds, there are many others. Start by looking in your local library or local museums. Your material could form the basis of a class display.

5 ☆ Invite someone from your local museum to come and talk to the class about recent local discoveries and investigations.

REMINDER - Complex Sentences.

In order to find out exactly what happened, and why the discovery remained a secret for three years, you will have to read Roald Dahl's story. But you know already that Ford was cleverer than Butcher and understood how valuable the find was, whereas Butcher did not. There are a number of things that Ford might do. However, anything he does would have consequences. We can express the consequences of Ford's actions by writing COMPLEX sentences using the words "if" and "then".
E.g. If he loses the treasure then he will be disappointed.
You may sometimes leave out the word, "then".
E.g. If he loses the treasure he will be disappointed.

Complete the following sentences to describe the consequences of certain courses of action.

If Ford reports the find to the authorities ...
If he keeps the treasure ...
If he tries to sell the treasure ...
If he goes back to the field and looks for more treasure ...
If he tells the owner of the field about the treasure ...

More treasure from Sutton Hoo.

SIGNIFICANCE

The significance of something - its meaning or importance - is not always obvious. The secret of making successful discoveries lies in noticing possibilities. If you see a possible significance then you explore further. Often it will lead nowhere, but occasionally people find something important.

Now try . . . . . .

6   Imagine you work in a museum and people often bring in things they have found. One of your jobs is to decide which finds are worth investigating further, and which are not. Remember - you are looking for things of interest to a museum, not just valuables.

The following six articles have been brought to you.

1. A large, iron nail, looks very old, probably hand-made. Found in a farmyard.
2. A very old silver coin with date worn away. Found in corner of field.
3. Some old photographs, one with date 1907. Found in attic of old house.
4. Piece of very old pottery, looks like the bottom of an earthenware jug with foreign markings on it. Found in back garden.
5. A very large, ancient iron key. Found by man digging in an allotment.
6. Some fragments of stained glass. Found in a cellar.

Your boss has told you to write short notes on each, saying whether you think they are important finds or not. You have to select ONE for investigation, and you must give reasons for your choice. In pairs, prepare your notes.

Hidden treasure is, of course, LITERALLY hidden. But we also speak figuratively of people having hidden talents. A previously unknown footballer may be suddenly "discovered", or a young child may be found to have a real talent for ice-skating. Some people think that EVERYONE has a talent of some sort. But not everyone discovers what their real talents are. Questionnaires have been produced to help people to find out more about themselves. The idea is that if you understand yourself better, you are more likely to make choices that will suit you, and to discover what are your talents.

 The following is a very simple questionnaire. For Section A you need to rule three columns on your paper, then number the statements and tick your response to each one. For Section B copy out the opening words and complete the sentence on your paper. You need not show your responses to anyone else if you do not wish to do so.

WHAT SORT OF PERSON AM I?

Complete this questionnaire as quickly as you can. Do not spend long thinking about each item, but put down your first reaction.

SECTION A

For each item, tick the column which is most true about you.

	Yes	Maybe	Not at all
1. I am good at practical subjects			
2. I am good at written work			
3. I find school work easy			
4. I do as I am told at school			
5. I am a bit of a rebel at school			
6. I like to look older than I am			
7. I am very active			
8. I make friends easily			
9. I always join in things			
10. I like to be on my own			
11. I always say what I think			
12. I lose my temper easily			
13. I enjoy challenges			
14. I don't give up easily			

SECTION B

Complete the following sentences. Do not think long about them, but put down the first idea that comes into your head.

1. I enjoy _____

2. I would like _____

3. I find difficult _____

4. I worry about _____

5. Other people think of me as _____

6. When I am older I want _____

_____

7. I hate _____

8. I think it is fun to _____

9. I wish my school _____

10. If there were one thing about my life that I could change it would be _____

_____

_____

If you wish, write two more sentences about yourself. You need not show these to anyone at this point.

Now try . . . . . .

1
- EITHER exchange your responses to the questionnaire with a friend.
- OR using your own responses to the questionnaire write a reference for yourself or your friend using only the information contained in the responses.
- The prospective employer will want to know about the applicant as a person. It is your task to be as positive as you can.

2 Design your own questionnaire which asks other important questions and fill it in yourself. Make any alterations to the questionnaire that you think are needed and then try it out on someone else.

3 Copy out one of the following passages and then continue it into a complete story. Give your story a title.

(a) As I opened the attic door I realised that no one had been in there for years and years. The light from the cobweb-covered window was just enough for me to see that everything was covered by a thick layer of dust.

(b) I had begun to think that I would never be any good at anything. But last Tuesday changed all that.

In this unit you will be looking at dialects and how languages change and develop. You will also be experimenting with some writing techniques.

LETTY MARE FIT TIFFY WONSIT. ZARF TRAWLY ZONIER KID.

If you cannot understand that, try reading it out loud. It comes from a book called *Let's Talk Strine* by Afferbeck Lauder, as do all the other examples of Strine. In the book, Lauder finds a way of writing which represents how Australians pronounce English. He does this by spelling the words phonetically - as they sound in a strong Australian accent.

(1) In pairs, read out the following conversation.

A. Sell semmitches?
B. Air, emeny jiwant?
A. Gimmee utter martyr and an airman pickle. Emma chisit?

Now try translating the following.

Euro merli. *(wife to husband)*
Split nair dyke - smor niken bear *(need an aspirin?)*
Watsy effris tea?
Aorta mica laura genst it.

ROO' STEAKS FOR TEA.

Now try . . . . . .

3 You may find it easier to do the following in pairs.
- Take any accent or dialect with which you are familiar. Write down some of the common words and phrases used, but spell them phonetically - as they would be pronounced. Then make up your own dictionary of 20-30 words and phrases, with explanations in English.
- Write out a conversation in dialect with all words spelt phonetically. Try it out in pairs before you write anything down, and read out your conversation to the rest of the class.
- Try tape-recording people in your area who speak with a pronounced accent. Write out some of their expressions phonetically.

(2) Imagine what would happen if words changed their spelling as their pronunciation was changed. It wouldn't take long for Strine to become a language quite different from English. Afferbeck Lauder thinks it is already! *Let's Talk Strine* is in fact a Strine English dictionary in which phonetic Strine words and phrases are explained in English. Here are some more extracts. (Answers on page 96.)

Air fridge - *ordinary.*
Baked necks, emma necks, scremblex - *popular breakfast dishes.*
Cheque etcher - *did you obtain.* As in: "Where cheque etcher hat?"
Egg jelly - *in fact, really.*
Sander's lape - *in a state of suspended animation.*

BAAAA.

You can see how different languages can develop from the same original language. Different accents develop which change into dialects and finally become so different as to be recognisable as different languages. Most languages you will hear in Europe have descended from the same original language which existed thousands of years ago.

(4) Languages steal words from each other. If you go to France, you may find they have taken some English words into their language quite recently. Examples are "le fast-food" and "le football". Can you think of any others? Or words which we have recently taken from other languages?

In the English language we have countless words adapted from other languages. Many of these are taken from Ancient Greek or Latin words, but there are plenty from other languages too.

(5) ☆ Try this word quiz. You will need a reasonably good dictionary for it. Rule out 5 columns as in the table below. Then copy out the list and fill in the gaps.

Original Word	Meaning	Original Language	Meaning of English Word	English Word
biblos	book	Greek	most famous book	
helix	wing		flying machine	
avis	bird		large cage for keeping birds	
rota	wheel		move in circular motion	
calculare	to work out in mathematics		to work out in mathematics	
roder	to gnaw		small, gnawing animal	
lamina	thin layer		to stick thin layers together	
psyche	mind		person who studies the mind	
promener	to walk		paved, seaside public place	
kinder	children		class for young children	
vagor	to wander		a wanderer with no home	
mono	alone		a single eyeglass	
escalier	stairs		moving staircase	
stethos	breast		heart and lung instrument	
suffah	cushion	Arabic	long seat with cushions	
robota	work		machine for repetitive tasks	
radix	root		edible root vegetable	
vacca	cow		to protect from disease	
jangal	overgrown waste ground	Hindi	tropical area of dense growth	
femme	woman		like a woman	
ta	to paint		to paint the skin	
shahmata	the king is dead		end of chess game	

Unfortunately for you, not all words in the English language are spelt *phonetically* - as they sound ...

Hints on Pronunciation for Foreigners

I take it you already know
Of tough and bough and cough and dough?
Others may stumble but not you,
On hiccough, thorough, lough and through?
Well done! And now you wish, perhaps,
To learn of less familiar traps?
Beware of heard, a dreadful word
That looks like beard and sounds like bird,
And dead: it's said like bed, not bead -
For goodness sake don't call it "deed"!
Watch out for meat and great and threat
(They rhyme with suite and straight and debt.)
A moth is not a moth in mother
Nor both in bother, broth in brother,
And here is not a match for there
Nor dear and fear for bear and pear,
And then there's dose and rose and lose
Just look them up - and goose and choose,
And cork and work and card and ward,
And font and front and word and sword,
And do and go and thwart and cart
Come, come, I've hardly made a start!
A dreadful language? Man alive!
I'd mastered it when I was five!

T.S.W

bough, *bow*,
cough, *kof*,
dough, *dō*,
hough, *hok*,
lough, *lohh*,
tough, *tuf*,

ugh, *uhh*,

You can see that we have words which are SPELT in a similar way but are PRONOUNCED differently, for example, *through, tough, bough* and *cough*. We also have words which are PRONOUNCED the same but are SPELT differently, for example, *great, straight, late* and *freight*.

(1) Make two lists, headed SAME SPELLING PATTERN but different sound and SAME SOUND but different spelling pattern.
☆

(2) Using a dictionary and with a time limit (say, 20 minutes), write down as many combinations of two or more words as you can under each heading. Make a class wall display, and add to it as you find other examples.

Now try . . . . . .

3 Here is a spelling game you can play with the entire class, or in groups of six or so.
In turn, each person calls out a letter. The letter combinations MUST be capable of building up to a word (Two-letter words don't count). But the person who completes a word by supplying the last letter is OUT. So anyone in danger of completing a word has three options.
1. They complete the word and are OUT.
2. They change the word being spelt. For example, if the sequence was C-H-A-N-G, then E would complete the word. So the next person might say I (having CHANGING in mind).
3. They might bluff, by calling out a letter which does not lead on to a word. If the next person calls their bluff, they are OUT. But if, for example, the next person could not think of a word going on from CHANGI, and challenged the previous person, then the challenger would be OUT. Continue the game until only one person is left.

"I'M SORRY, THAT'S NOT QUITE WHAT I MEANT."

It is easy to slip up in talk or writing. Everyone does it sometimes, particularly if they feel under pressure of some sort.

Sports commentators on television have become famous for their errors, and it is easy to understand why. When they are describing moments of great excitement, they become caught up in them and have not time to think carefully about what they are saying. Also, sports have their own specialist languages and when that is combined with English, the two can become mixed. Think of all the technical language in cricket where the words have quite different meanings in ordinary English: *short leg; maiden; silly mid-on; fine leg.*

"The forwards shot hard and often. At last he decided to try his head. It came off first time."

"When the baby has finished its bottle, it must be washed. If the baby does not like fresh milk, it should be boiled."

"That's a definite maybe ... we'd better go on before we go any further."

Another group of people famous for slips under pressure is yourselves. School students writing in examinations have produced so many unintentional errors the Examination Boards often print a selection when the Fifth Year examinations have been marked. These have been called "Howlers" for many years. However, it is not just school students. School teachers are also famous for their unintentional slips, whether on formal occasions like assemblies or in comments on students' work. No one can escape!

Writers through the ages have invented characters who misuse the language in some way or other. One of the most famous is Mrs Malaprop in Sheridan's play, *The Rivals*. She has a habit of replacing the correct word with one that is similar, but which means something quite different. Because of her, this kind of mistake is called a "malapropism". Many, though not all, howlers are malapropisms.

"Illiterate him, I say, quite from your memory."

(4) Using the examples on this page as a basis for a collection, add to them in all 4 categories. You can collect real ones and invent some as well. You could also make a class collection of the best.

Now try . . . . . .

5 Write an entire speech for a sports commentator or a headteacher, filling it with appropriate errors. You could try this once you have collected a good few examples.

6 Write a short piece of dialogue including
☆ Mrs Malaprop and other characters which you invent.

11.3 Becoming a Writer.

There are plenty of easy techniques and ideas which will improve your writing, but like everything else, good writing needs practice. Try the following.

(1) VARIATIONS ON A THEME
Choose an incident - something that has happened to you in the past. Now write down the incident, using the first person (I) and the past tense. Keep it short - just a bare outline of 3 or 4 sentences. This is your *theme* and you can play some variations on it. There is no need to do all that is suggested - some might not be effective for your chosen theme. Invent more variations of your own to try as well.

- Rewrite your story in the present tense.
- Rewrite your story in the second person ('you' instead of 'I').
- Rewrite your story in the third person ('he', 'she', 'they' for 'I', and 'we').

- Rewrite using the third person but changing the sexes of all the characters.
- Retell the incident as if it were being told by someone else in the story.
- Retell the story as if you were a witness who had seen it happen and was being questioned about it.

- Retell the story using only nouns (this will be ungrammatical, but you should be able to understand it!).
- Choose ONE character in the story and write down as many adjectives as you can to describe what that person felt.
- Imagine you are able to look back in time and see the incident happening now. Write down the comments you might make.

- Write out the incident as a script for a radio play (remember, NO NARRATOR, so you must tell the story through sounds and speech).
- Tell the story using no adjectives or adverbs.
- Choose an important word or group of words from your first account. Write down all the words or phrases that come into your head as you think about it. Can you rearrange these effectively?

(2) Now ask yourself the following questions.
- Which is the best piece of writing that came out of that exercise?
- Which did you find the most difficult to do?
- Which did you find the easiest?

USING A MODEL.

Dylan Thomas was a Welsh poet and writer who wrote very vividly about his childhood. In his time, August Bank Holiday was always the first Monday in August, not the last, so it really felt like a beginning. The following extract comes from his autobiographical essay, *Holiday Memory*.

August Bank Holiday. A tune on an ice-cream cornet. A slap of sea and a tickle of sand. A fanfare of sunshades opening. A wince and whinny of bathers dancing into deceptive water. A tuck of dresses. A rolling of trousers. A compromise of paddlers. A sunburn of girls and a lark of boys. A silent hullabaloo of balloons.

I remember the sea telling lies in a shell held to my ear for a whole harmonious, hollow minute by a small, wet girl in an enormous bathing-suit marked "Corporation Property".

I remember sharing the last of my moist buns with a boy and a lion. Tawny and savage, with cruel nails and capacious mouth, the little boy tore and devoured. Wild as a seed-cake, ferocious as a hearth-rug, the depressed and verminous lion nibbled like a mouse at his half a bun, and hiccupped in the sad dusk of his cage.

Children all day capered or squealed by the glazed or bashing sea, and the steam-organ wheezed its waltzes in the threadbare playground and the waste lot, where the dodgems dodged, behind the pickle factory.

And mothers loudly warned their proud pink daughters or sons to put that jellyfish down; and fathers spread newspapers over their faces; and sand-fleas hopped on the picnic lettuce; and someone had forgotten the salt.

In those always radiant, rainless, lazily rowdy and sky-blue summers departed, I remember August Monday from the rising of the sun over the stained and royal town to the husky hushing of the roundabout music and the drowsing of the naphtha jets in the seaside fair: from bubble-and-squeak to the last of the sandy sandwiches.

There was no need, that holiday morning, for the sluggardly boys to be shouted down to breakfast; out of their jumbled beds they tumbled, scrambled into their rumpled clothes; quickly at the bathroom basin they catlicked their hands and faces, but never forgot to run the water loud and long as though they washed like colliers; in front of the cracked looking-glass bordered with cigarette cards, in their treasure-trove bedrooms, they whisked a gap-tooth comb through their surly hair; and with shining cheeks and noses and tide-marked necks, they took the stairs three at a time.

But for all their scramble and scamper, clamour on the landing, catlick and toothbrush flick, hair-whisk and stair-jump, their sisters were always there before them. Up with the lady lark, they had prinked and frizzed and hot-ironed; and smug in their blossoming dresses, ribboned for the sun, in gym-shoes white as the blanco'd snow, neat and silly with doilies and tomatoes they helped in the higgledy kitchen. They were calm; they were virtuous; they had washed their necks; they did not romp, or fidget; and only the smallest sister put out her tongue at the noisy boys.

(3) Imagine an open-air market. Shut your eyes to see it, hear it, and smell it more vividly. Then, write down, as fast as you can, words which give an impression of the sights, sounds, and smells of your market.

- Write about the market copying Dylan Thomas's style. Let the words tumble out in a rush. Invent new words - but you must understand them; join words together, too.
- Write your first paragraph. Notice Dylan Thomas has NO FINITE VERBS in the entire paragraph. He just lists his impressions. Do the same for yours.
- Still using Thomas's passage as a model, write your next two paragraphs starting with the words "I remember".
- Lastly, continue with a few paragraphs describing some things that are happening in the market.

Show, not tell! You have probably been told this before, but it is important! Compare these two passages.

Passage A

Duncan walked out of the school gate in the semi-darkness and picked up a stone. After a quick look round, he scraped the sharp edge fiercely across the headmaster's name on the school board. Then he half turned, flung the stone towards the school buildings, and dashed out into the street, ignoring the hoot of a car as the driver braked sharply to avoid him.

The darkening gloom of the evening exactly mirrored his mood. He had only been at his new comprehensive a few weeks but already he felt he had lost all his old friends and made no new ones. Today had been the last straw. A scuffle on the bus had been followed by a complaint to the headmaster and he had been picked out - he, who had only retaliated to defend himself. As a result, after an hour's detention, he had missed the bus and had to walk home.

He slowed down as he reached the factory alongside the school. As he expected, the foul smell from the processing plant hung, heavy in the cool evening air. He could actually taste the fumes. It was, he felt, the school's fault he was being forced to breathe this poison.

Without thinking, he kicked a stone through the fencing and, hearing a crash, ran on again towards the level crossing.

He arrived there just as the gates were shutting. As he was climbing over he heard a warning shout from the signalman. He looked up, punched a two-finger sign into the air and ran across the rails, over the other gate, and away down the road.

Passage B

Duncan felt angry and frustrated. He was furious at being treated unfairly, and he had no friends. He felt he hated everyone and everyone hated him. The whole world seemed to be against him and all he could do was to take his revenge in any way he could, by being rude and unpleasant. There was no one for him to talk it over with, and his angry energy was building up inside him. Even people trying to help could only expect an aggressive response.

Now try ......

1 In Passage A, we are SHOWN exactly what happens and we can enter into the feelings of the boy. In Passage B we are merely TOLD how he feels and reacts. Which do you find the more interesting? If these were openings to a story, which one would you be more likely to continue?

2 ☆ In each case you are given (1) the bare facts of the incident, and (2) the feelings it caused. Your task is to write the story of one of them, making up any details you wish in order to make the story come alive. Do NOT tell how it felt. Instead, make sure you SHOW exactly what happened. Use first or third person as you wish.

(1) Crossing road. Fast car suddenly comes round corner. Squealing of tyres and brakes. Just misses.
(2) Concern - fear - terror relief - shock.
(1) Out walking in open country. Sun turns to wind and rain. Reach isolated cafe.
(2) Happy, carefree - miserably wet and cold - relief and comfort.

This poem was written by a contemporary poet from Nottingham, Sherile Turner. Many famous British poets have written mainly dialect poetry - for example, Robert Burns in Scotland. Like most dialect poetry, it is meant to be read out loud.

De Steel Band

De other day mi go to a show
An mi eyes dem pop out so
Mi see di kids dem play ina one steel band
An dem bang an bang pon di pan

Mi caan member di name of di show
But it go something like
Pan-de, pan-de, pan-de-mo

Mi just a sit down deh
Ina mi seat
It was velvet too
An one o di time mi feel seh mi wan fi Do-Do
But no toilet de-deh
So mi just sit down an stare

Mi sit down deh a watch dem
An mi member di name was
PANDEMONIEM

After all dis time de name come to me
An det deh time me did wan fi wee-wee
Den dem ha di singing from de choir
An di lights dem tun red as fire

Dem sing some song
From de play name Cats
An wen di cats dem come on
Mi did tink seh dem a bats

Den after dat we ave a break
An de noise it gi me headache
Den wi hab another steel ban
Dem was di star o di show
Fa dem come from Trinidad you know!

Me seh dem play some groovy song
An me seh dem nice and dem long
Mi seh one o buoy dem deh a di back
Mi never see nobody drop foot like dat

Dem play Lionel Richie's song
It name you is or you are
An tru dem come from so far
Dem play Jamaica Rombus
An me start fe sing

Dem mek whole heap a fuss
Den wi hear one more song
An me tell you seh di trip didn't long
Cause den wi haffe go home
But me hope seh dem will come back soon.

Sherile Turner

3 Read the poem aloud. If you are not familiar with this dialect, you may need to discuss some parts to understand it fully. This is a real dialect which sometimes constructs sentences in ways different from Standard English. For example, look at the use of "dem" in Lines 2 and 3, where in Standard English no word would be used.

4 Go through the poem and note where the language construction is different from Standard English.

Now try . . . . . .

5 Try writing a poem in dialect of your own choice. You could write about something lively like a disco, but if you have other ideas, use them.

12.1 Own Reading.

In this unit you will be looking at your own reading choices and those of others. You will also be doing some research.

(1) The following questionnaire is about reading choices. If each person in the class answers all the questions, the results could form the basis of a discussion. You might also want to summarise the answers to each question. If you decide to do the latter, it would be a good idea for everyone to write their answers on sheets of paper, not in exercise books; then these could be cut up, and the task of making summaries to answers could be shared out.

HOW DO YOU READ?

1. Do you read for pleasure
   every day/every week/ occasionally/ never? _____

2. Do you use a library?
   If so, which one(s)? _____

3. What do you enjoy reading most? _____

4. When in the day do you most like to read? _____

5. If you can, where do you choose to go to read? _____

6. Can you remember, roughly, how many novels
   you have read during the last month or so?
   If you can, how many was it? _____

7. If someone were to ask you to recommend a book
   for a good read, what would you recommend? _____

8. Why? _____

9. Do you read magazines or comics
   often/sometimes/never? _____

10. Which ones do you read often or sometimes? _____

11. Do you feel that you are well-served by
    libraries and bookshops in your area? _____

12. Do you have any suggestions for improvement in
    library and bookshop provision where you live? _____

LIBRARY RESEARCH.

As soon as a subject becomes a matter of publicity or public concern and interest, publishers compete with each other to get books out about it as fast as possible. In that way, they hope to sell a lot quickly and make a great deal of money. For example, when a new Pop or Soap Opera Star appears, the shops soon fill up with pictures, magazines about him or her, calendars, books, and so on. Then, someone else becomes famous, and everyone forgets about "yesterday's star". All the pictures, books and so on are "remaindered" - that is, sold off cheaply - and no one wants to buy them!

But some issues are important, even if they are not always in the news. Our society in Britain is a multi-cultural society and we are concerned about the environment and equality of opportunity for girls as well as boys. There are three important issues which are not going to go away.

1. Living together in a multi-cultural society.
2. Caring for our environment.
3. Equal opportunities for girls and boys.

(2) Add three other important issues of today to this list.

Our libraries should contain books about the important issues of today. But these change from time to time, and it is not easy to keep up to date. However, you are entitled to have access to such books, fiction as well as non-fiction. These issues, our three plus any you have added, can form the basis of your study.

(3) As a class, investigate what is available to you that deals with these issues. You will need to work in small groups. First choose an issue to investigate; that is your subject. Make sure that ALL the issues are covered by your class. Investigate how well your subject is covered in books and magazines available to you.

(4) ☆ Once your group knows which subject you are covering, you will need to find out the following.
1. What books can you find in the School Library Non-Fiction section on your subject?
2. What books can you find in the School Library Fiction section on your subject?
3. If possible, do the same for your local Public Library.
4. How well do local bookshops cover your subject?
5. What magazines are there, if any, which are concerned about your subject?
6. Publishers send out lots of material advertising their up to date books and magazines. If you can, get hold of some and find out if your subject is being covered adequately. The School Library might be able to help.

Now try . . . . . .

5 Choose a short story or an article which is to do with your subject, and make a special study of that. Ask the following questions about it, and try to answer them, with your reasons. Think up questions of your own.
- Is it well-informed?
- Is it fair?
- Is it easily understandable?
- Do you agree with what is being said about your subject?
- Does it make you think?

6 All the groups in the class will have found out a great deal.
- Make displays of what you have found, or each group could give a presentation to the rest of the class.
- If you choose the latter, do not try to cover everything you have found. Pick out two or three points to make which you could explain and then encourage discussion of them.

12.2 Areas of Research.

Most of your reading will not be of books at all, but *ephemera* - that is, writing that is not intended to last. This category includes magazines, comics, newspapers, advertisements, school notices, notes passed round the class, and so on.

WHAT MAGAZINES DO YOU READ?
Carry out a quick class survey. Each of you write down up to 5 magazines or comics that you read most often. Do this without discussion, so that you get a reliable list. List them all, with numbers of students who named them. Next lesson, make sure at least one copy of each is brought in.

CONTENTS SURVEY. ☆
In groups, carry out a Contents Survey of each of the more popular magazines, for display. You will need to share out this task, taking one magazine each. Work out what the different contents are, first editorial, articles, letters, stories, advertisements, and so on. Then work out how many pages there are of each kind. Write your findings on a sheet of paper so that they can all be displayed.

UNUSUAL CHOICES.
Arrange for anyone who was the ONLY person to mention a particular magazine to give a talk about it, explaining why they find that one interesting.

SHARING.
Magazines are expensive. Why not come to a class arrangement so that you have a kind of Class Magazine Library, regularly updated with the latest editions? Between you, it may well be possible to collect numbers of some magazines regularly at little or no cost, and if these were made available, all could share them.

COMMERCIAL BREAK.
Most magazines publish letters from their readers. Most pay quite handsomely for them, especially for "Letter of the Month" or similar feature. Make a serious study of the kind of letters accepted in your chosen magazine, and write a letter to send in. Unless your class is singularly unfortunate, some will be printed, and some will receive payment.

AUTHORS.
Who are the favourite authors in your class? Are they the same authors as the School librarian, or your local librarian recommends? Ask them for their recommendations and compare them with your choices.

LOCAL AUTHORS.
Wherever you are in the country, there will be several authors living in your area, including some who specialise in writing for young people. Seek them out and invite them in to talk to your class and answer questions. Your local Library or Arts Centre should be able to help you to trace these authors. You will find that most authors welcome this kind of contact - after all, they WANT their books to be read! It would be a good idea to make sure that some members of the class had read some of the author's books before she or he comes to talk to you.

FICTION
NOVELS ARRANGED IN ALPHABETICAL ORDER OF THEIR AUTHORS

HISTORY
BOOKS ABOUT THE PAST

BIOGRAPHY
LIVES OF FAMOUS PEOPLE

TRAVEL
BOOKS ABOUT DIFFERENT COUNTRIES

PHILOSOPHY
BOOKS BY FAMOUS THINKERS LIKE ARISTOTLE

RELIGION
BOOKS ABOUT THE BIBLE CHRISTIANITY AND DIFFERENT BELIEFS

SUBJECTS.
What subjects do you like to read about? Are they the same as those that your friends would choose? Why do you like these subjects? Can you write a story about one of your favourite subjects which YOU would want to read, had you not written it? You might need to do some research first so that your story is authentic.

RECOMMENDED AUTHORS.
Individually, or in pairs, produce a poster recommending the books of your chosen author. The aim of these posters is to encourage others to read books by this author. Approach the task through the following stages.
- Choose which author to publicise. It need not be your favourite one - but one you would recommend. Try to ensure that together the whole class covers a good range.
- Find out the publisher that publishes the books of your chosen author. You will need to get hold of a copy of that publisher's catalogue. This should not be difficult. Such catalogues are free, and readily available. You could get one from your own School Library, the local Public Library, a bookshop, or even by writing to the publisher.
- List as many books by your author as you can, and get hold of some of them. Read and look through some of his/her work.
- Make a quick list of the features of this author which you like, and which you are going to highlight. For example, you might enjoy the subjects of the books, or the excitement in them, or possibly particular characters.
- Start work on the poster, highlighting what you have discovered, and making it as attractive and inviting as possible.

Acknowledgements

Folens Publishers would like to thank the following authors and publishers for permission to reproduce their material:

Passage about Jacob from *Words 3* by Richard Andrews and Geoffrey Summerfield, published by Cassell.
A Martian Sends a Postcard Home from *A Martian Sends a Postcard Home* by Craig Raine (1979). Reprinted by permission of Oxford University Press.
Lizzie from *Quickly Let's Get Out of Here* by Michael Rosen. Andre Deutsch Ltd.
2 Young 2 Go 4 Grils from *Kill-A-Louse Week* by Susan Gregory (Viking Kestrel, 1986), copyright Susan Gregory, 1986.
Passage from *The Vertical Ladder* by William Sansom, copyright William Sansom, 1948. Permission granted by Elaine Greene Ltd.
Tom Colley's Ghost from *World of the Unknown: Ghosts.* Reproduced by permission of Usborne Publishing Ltd.
Durham to London train timetable, courtesy of British Rail.
By-pass leaflet Crown copyright, reproduced with the permission of the Controller of Her Majesty's Stationery Office.
Sea-Coal by Robert Westall. Copyright Robert Westall.
Passage from *What Society Does To Girls* by Joyce Nicholson, reproduced by permission of Longman Cheshire Pty Limited, Australia.
Who's Afraid by Philippa Pearce. Copyright 1978 Philippa Pearce from *Who's Afraid*, Puffin books. Permission granted by the author.
My Sister Jane by Ted Hughes. Reprinted by permission of Faber and Faber Ltd from *Meet My Folks* by Ted Hughes.
Passage from *Claudine*, originally *Claudine A l'Ecole* by Colette translated by Antonia White. Reprinted by permission of Martin Secker and Warburg.
Passage from *The Mildenhall Treasure* by Roald Dahl from *The Wonderful Story of Henry Sugar*, Jonathan Cape Ltd and Penguin Books Ltd. Copyright 1977 by Roald Dahl.
Passages from *Beowulf*, translated by Kevin Crossley-Holland, copyright the author. Macmillan 1968.
Extracts from *Let's Talk Strine* by Afferbeck Lauder, courtesy of Weldon Publishing, Sydney, Australia.
Passage from *Holiday Memory* by Dylan Thomas, courtesy of the publishers of *The Collected Stories*, J M Dent.

PHOTOGRAPHS

Folens Publishers would like to acknowledge:
The Trustees of the British Museum (Page 4, 76, 77, 78, 81).
Jan and Jim Crawley (Page 7).
Linda Robson (Page 37, 39, 53,).
Eileen and Terry Brown (Page 68).
Beamish, The North of England Open Air Museum, Durham (page 40).

ILLUSTRATORS

Philip Hodgson, Sal Shuel, Paul Bevan, Eric Jones, Toni Moore.
Cover design by Tanglewood Graphics, Broadway House, The Broadway, London SW19. Tel: O1 543 3048.
Cover illustration by Abacus Publicity Ltd.

Folens Publishers have made every effort to contact copyright holders but this has not always been possible. If any have been overlooked we will be pleased to make any necessary arrangements.

ANSWERS

Page 7
A = a Primary School Head Teacher. Did you expect a Head Teacher to be male? Did you expect a teacher to be cross?
B = a teacher. She looks happy enough!
C = a doctor. What do you expect a doctor to look like? This one is obviously looking thoughtful.

Page 23
Claustrophobia = fear of enclosed spaces; agoraphobia = fear of open spaces; bibliophobia = fear of books; clinophobia = fear of going to bed; hydrophobia = fear of water; necrophobia = fear of death; stasiphobia = fear of standing up; ornithophobia = fear of birds; ophidiophobia = fear of snakes; halophobia = fear of speaking; entomophobia = fear of insects; hedonophobia = fear of pleasure.

Page 43
A = late fourteenth century. Chaucer - *Prologue to the Canterbury Tales*. Costume (d).
B = 1850. Charles Dickens - *David Copperfield*. Costume (c).
C = 1766. Oliver Goldsmith - *The Vicar of Wakefield*. Costume (a).
D = 1834. Honore de Balzac - *Old Father Goriot*. (Translated late nineteenth century). Costume (c).

Page 77
The Law of Treasure Trove.
This ancient law applies only to finds of gold or silver and not to other metals. It is still in force today.
The law states that if a person digs any gold or silver out of the ground, it is automatically known as Treasure Trove and becomes the property of the crown. Nowadays, the "Crown" means country or government. The finder MUST report any such find and, on doing so, he or she is entitled to receive from the government the full amount of the market price of the find in money.
The owner of the land gets nothing - unless the finder was trespassing at the time.

Page 84
1. "Do you sell sandwiches?"
    "Yes. How many do you want?"
    "Give me a tomato and a ham and pickle. How much is it?"

    "You're home early."
    Splitting headache.
    "What does he have for his tea?"
    They ought to make a law against it.

2. Average; bacon and eggs, ham and eggs, scrambled eggs; did you get your ..; actually; sound asleep.

Page 85
Reading down the "Original language" column:
Greek; Greek; Latin; Latin; Latin; Latin; Latin; Greek; French; German; Latin; Greek; French; Greek; Arabic; Czech; Latin; Latin; Hindi; French; Maori; Persian.
Reading down the "English Word" column:
Bible; helicopter; aviary; rotate; calculate; rodent; laminate; psychologist; promenade; kindergarten; vagrant; monocle; escalator; stethoscope; sofa; robot; radish; vaccinate; jungle; feminine; tattoo; check-mate.